To

Tom

Best wishes

from

THE LITTLE RED BOOK OF
LIVERPOOL
FC

THE LITTLE RED BOOK OF
LIVERPOOL
FC

DARREN PHILLIPS

First published 2010

The History Press
The Mill, Brimscombe Port
Stroud, Gloucestershire, GL5 2QG
www.thehistorypress.co.uk

British Library Cataloguing in Publication Data.
A catalogue record for this book is available from the British
Library.

ISBN 978 0 7524 5441 2

Typesetting and origination by The History Press
Printed in Great Britain
Manufacturing managed by Jellyfish Print Solutions Ltd

ACKNOWLEDGEMENTS

Writing any book, no matter what the subject or length, can be an onerous task. It takes a huge number of hours to research and then, shoulders hunched over a keyboard, commit some words to screen. However, any Liverpool fan would jump at the chance to do nothing more than write about their club – especially as delving through almost 120 years of history plus scrapbooks, programmes and other ephemera does at least create a diversion from the more meagre fare of recent years.

There is real satisfaction gained from learning more about the people and events which have made Liverpool Football Club the institution that it is and always will be. No matter what lies ahead, it is hoped that leafing through the pages of this book will make the reader feel the same emotions.

Though the thanks to follow will be brief they are no less heartfelt because of that. A debt of gratitude is due to all at The History Press for their professionalism but especially Michelle Tilling for approaching me about the project and help throughout the writing and editorial process. Then there are the invaluable people at lfchistory.net. No matter how well any Red may know their club as a subject, or the depth of records journalists tend to hoard, their tireless work ensures a vital resource to check against.

ACKNOWLEDGMENTS

IN THE BEGINNING THERE WAS . . . EVERTON

Although Liverpool Football Club and Anfield are names inextricably linked with each other, Everton were the first team to call the stadium home. Only when a row over the rental costs and unease about some of the business interests of landowner (and their president) John Houlding came to a head in 1892 did the club move away. As a consequence, Anfield no longer had a team to occupy it, so Houlding formed his own club.

It cost £6,000 to buy the land. The rental charge at the beginning of the tenancy in 1884 had more than doubled within five years to reach £250 per annum. The majority of the Everton board wanted to offer no more than £180 each year. Though this issue was key in the exit, so too was Houlding's desire to sell his own ales at the ground. Some of his boardroom colleagues were Methodists who saw temperance as a virtue. Other factors included an insistence that the players change at his Sandon Hotel public house on Oakfield Road despite it being the best part of 100 metres away from the pitch and meaning players would have to make their way through crowds before each home game.

Brewing was a huge part of Houlding's business empire and the Sandon, which still stands, for many years acted as an administrative headquarters for the club as well as a trophy room. Meetings were held in the bowls pavilion at the back of the establishment and many team photographs were posed for in front of the same building.

The stadium's first competitive game saw Everton beat Earlestown 5–0 on 28 September 1884. Liverpool's debut came in a friendly with Rotherham United on 1 September 1892, the Yorkshiremen finding themselves on the wrong end of a 7–1 scoreline. Two days later Higher Walton were thrashed 8–0 in the Lancashire League. Liverpool's first Football League game at Anfield came on 9 September 1893 when Lincoln City were soundly beaten 4–0.

LIVERPOOL FC – 19 TIMES CHAMPIONS OF ENGLAND

At present Liverpool are tied with Manchester United on 18 league titles; a mark they set in 1990 and the Red Devils equalled in 2009. However, Liverpool Football Club have won one more championship than is officially accepted. When Everton left Anfield they could only do so by setting up a fresh company with a new board, directors and officials, plus the issue of 5,000 shares. The Football League allowed this entity to take the name and retain League membership. John Houlding, who after all was known as 'King John of Everton', wanted his new club to inherit all those privileges, but once this was denied he changed the club's name.

He registered 'Everton F.C. and Athletic Grounds Ltd' on 15 March 1892 while the soon-to-be old tenants remained in residence. Once that plan was thwarted the new name – intended to be Liverpool F.C. until the city's rugby team objected – Liverpool Football Club and Athletic Grounds Ltd was adopted. Towards the end of March, just two weeks after the board split, Houlding's committee passed a resolution giving effect to the suggestion. During the summer the Board of Trade, a government department, accepted the change of name from Everton Football Club and Athletic Grounds Company Ltd – who finished top of the league in 1891 – to Liverpool Football Club and Athletic Grounds Company Ltd.

The record books reflect that Everton FC hold that title and no Liverpool fan will want to claim the accolade but strictly speaking the Reds have won 19 English titles and are looking to reach 20 before their rivals.

NATIONAL SERVICE

Anfield was used for an England v Republic of Ireland 'B' International and then a Euro '96 qualifier involving the Republic and Holland in 1995. With England as hosts, Anfield also staged finals matches. Three group games involving Italy, the Czech Republic and Russia were played plus a quarter-final tie between France and Holland. Italy returned in September 1998 to take on Wales in a European Championships qualifier. Nine months later the Welsh were using it as a temporary home to play Denmark. Both games were staged in Liverpool under directives from UEFA as, with the old Cardiff Arms Park being transformed into the Millennium Stadium, each visiting federation suggested all stadiums in the principality were unable to cater for the large number of visiting fans. Wales lost 2–0 on each occasion and went down by the same scoreline when the ground was used as a neutral venue for a controversial World Cup finals eliminator in October 1977 between Scotland and Wales. Kenny Dalglish opened the scoring with a flicked header but the tie was made safe for the Tartan Army with a penalty awarded for hand ball. However, TV replays afterwards seemed to suggest that the hand making contact was that of Scottish striker Joe Jordan.

Anfield held the first of eight England International matches as far back as 1889 when the national team beat Ireland 6–1. The same opponents returned in 1926. Further games took place against Wales in 1905, 1922 and 1931. Finland, who had a World Cup qualifier in L4, are the only visitors to play a competitive fixture at Anfield outside the Home Championships. South American opponents came for friendlies while Wembley was being rebuilt with Paraguay welcomed in 2002, then Uruguay four years later.

THE HOME TEAM WAS MANCHESTER UNITED

It isn't often that a Manchester United side walks out at Anfield and receives a roaring ovation from the Kop. However, at the beginning of the 1971/72 season that's exactly what happened. Fans on the terrace clad in red and white were not Liverpudlians, though. United were banned from playing their first two home games either at their own ground or their next preference Maine Road as the previous term hooligans had hurled knives into the Old Trafford away section.

At the FA's direction those matches were played at Stoke City's Victoria Ground and Anfield – which would host the first of those fixtures against Arsenal. On Friday 20 August, 27,649 fans were in attendance with Liverpool taking 15 per cent of the gate. As the numbers were less than would be expected for a true home game, Arsenal received compensation for the expected shortfall in their share of receipts. Everton gained too, as attendance at their match a day later dropped below 46,000.

PERRY KOPS IT

Anfield has hosted its fair share of other sporting events; indeed the Liverpool Marathon had its finishing line in front of the Kop during the mid-1920s. Both rugby codes have been staged at the venue and boxing bouts were regular sights for many years. Perhaps the most talked about was Nel Tarleton's fight with Freddie Miller for the World Featherweight crown in 1934. Tarleton had already won and lost British titles at Anfield but failed to beat Miller, who was the holder.

A sport involving nets rather than knockouts – tennis – was played prior to the war years at which time the legendary Fred Perry, three-times winner of the All England Championship, graced the field. Boards were laid out on the pitch to create the playing area – the hallowed turf was not used. Stockport-born Perry decided that too little of his game was seen outside the plush environs of places like Wimbledon and set up exhibitions at various points around the country. Liverpool played host to the 1937 International Lawn Tennis Contest where Perry played American Ellsworth Vines who was ranked as the world's number one for a lengthy spell. Another US player to take on Britain's finest racquet man was Bill Tilden.

A NEW ANFIELD

In 2002, after 110 years of calling Anfield home, the Liverpool board mooted the possibility of moving from their famous stadium and building a new ground just 400 yards away on a site used by Everton over the first three years of their existence. Almost a decade on that has failed to transpire. Though the club remain committed to the development, they have only been able to carry out basic enabling works.

However, a move to another part of the city could have taken place in the late 1960s if one of Bill Shankly's ideas had been adopted. It may also have seen the Reds share with Everton. Both thoughts were certainly something Shanks was open to when suggesting that a purpose-built facility could be built in the Aintree district. Despite the renovations he had managed to push through, he felt neither Anfield nor Goodison were worthy of the fans who congregated there.

THE TEAM OF MACS

When Liverpool kicked off their debut season, they did so with no less than 13 Scots in a 19-man squad. The first 11 men to take the field only had 3 players from south of the border. Many stayed beyond that season and played League football. Among their number were Bill and Joe McQue from Celtic, Malcolm McVean who joined from Third Lanark, Matt and Hugh McQueen once of Leith Athletic, John McCartney who came via St Mirren, plus Duncan McLean and John McBride of Renton. The distinctive prefix from their surnames plus that Scottish bent meant Liverpool became known as 'The Team of Macs'.

BEFORE FOOTBALL

Not everyone has taken a route into football which involves playing their way through the grades. Years ago many young professionals, not to mention experienced ones, had to take jobs outside the game to make ends meet. Liverpool's roster includes a number of intriguing professions.

Ray Clemence	deck chair attendant
Billy Liddell	accountant
Ron Yeats	slaughterman
Jimmy Case	electrician
Matt Busby	miner
Sam English	shipyard worker
Brian Hall	bus conductor

STOLEN SILVER

Liverpool have won 43 major trophies but the very first pieces of silverware lifted – the 1893 Lancashire League and Liverpool Senior Cup captured at the end of the club's inaugural campaign – were stolen. They were displayed in a pawnshop owned by Charles Gibson in the Paddington area of the city. Presumably sold for scrap and melted down, they were never recovered leaving Liverpool with a £130 bill for replacements.

ANFIELD SOUTH

Wembley earned the nickname Anfield South among the Reds faithful due to the sheer number of visits paid there. Including both domestic cups, Charity Shields and the 1978 European Cup final, Liverpool had appeared at the national stadium 30 times before its closure in 2000. Since it was reopened in 2007, the Reds have yet to make a debut appearance.

MILESTONE GOALS – EUROPE

1	Gordon Wallace	v	KR Reykjavík	17 August 1964
100	Steve Heighway	v	Dynamo Berlin	13 December 1972
200	Emlyn Hughes	v	Anderlecht	19 December 1978
300	Dean Saunders	v	Swarowski Tirol	11 December 1992
400	Emile Heskey	v	Spartak Moscow	2 October 2002
500	Yossi Benayoun	v	Besiktas	6 November 2007

BRIGHT OPENINGS

Liverpool have opened campaigns with wins more times than any other club. When the Reds beat Sunderland in the first game of the 2008/09 season it meant that from 106 League campaigns (including the 2009/10 season) Liverpool had tasted victory on 62 occasions.

ARMCHAIR SPECTATORS

Liverpool have achieved many feats in front of television cameras – in fact the two have gone hand-in-hand for decades. Anfield hosted the first ever *Match of the Day* programme when the BBC brought highlights of the top-flight game against Arsenal on 22 August 1964. The Reds ran out 3–2 winners courtesy of a late Gordon Wallace goal. However, not everyone was able to see the game as it was screened on BBC2, a channel launched in April 1964 and not available throughout the UK for a number of years. When colour broadcasts were stepped up during the latter part of that decade, Liverpool led the way once more as Anfield hosted another first – a match with West Ham United not being shown in black and white! It allowed commentators to indicate that the team playing in red was Liverpool rather than just refer to directions of play.

In addition the Kop was the subject of a *Panorama* special which examined its history, effect on the Liverpool team and their opposition. Further documentaries charting the adventures of the club and its fans were made. These include *The Kop Flies East* – when a first trip was made behind the Iron Curtain to face Honved of Hungary.

At the time of the Premiership's foundation in 1992, the opening round of games was played on 15 August –

except one. Kept back for live broadcast 24 hours later by the rights holder Sky TV was Nottingham Forest against Liverpool. Teddy Sheringham got the only goal seen at the City Ground that afternoon and the first witnessed by a new breed of spectator.

Away from factual programming the club or its players have featured in a host of other broadcasts. *Scully*, penned by Alan Bleasdale and shown on Channel 4, was the story of a Kenny Dalglish-obsessed teenager desperate to earn a trial and hear the Kop chant his name. Dalglish made a number of guest appearances during the series. The Liverpool writer's breakthrough work as far as TV audiences were concerned, *Boys from the Black Stuff*, also aired during the 1980s. In one of the programmes Sammy Lee and Graeme Souness were present at a charity night during which the infamous character Yosser Hughes decided to introduce himself to the then Liverpool captain.

A well loved and at the same time often loathed character, Alf Garnett from the sitcom *In Sickness and in Health* attended a game between his beloved West Ham United and Liverpool at Anfield. The actor portraying him, Warren Mitchell, accompanied by the son-in-law he referred to as 'The Scouse Git' – Liverpool-born actor Tony Booth – featured in scenes shot during the game with players in the background as the two exchange banter.

PLAYING FOR TIME

When Derby County played Liverpool in December 1979 they earned a penalty just 20 seconds in. The Rams were top-flight strugglers and knew they were unlikely to hold off Bob Paisley's rampant side until the end, so with little more than a minute gone, they decided to wind the clock down. Roy McFarland took it on himself to make the first of many efforts to waste time and attempted to find 'row Z' with a boot into the stands. The referee issued a yellow card which the England man sat on for roughly 88 minutes.

BOGEY TEAMS – FOXES AND SEAGULLS HAUNT LIVERBIRD

Despite beating the best England and Europe had to offer for many years, there were always teams the Reds could not seem to conquer. In the 1960s it was Leicester City. The Foxes were firmly established in the top flight when Liverpool achieved promotion in 1962. Of the first six League meetings after that, the Reds won just once. Leicester claimed the 1963 FA Cup semi-final tie between the two clubs when Gordon Banks was in great form. The Midlanders' fortunes slid soon after as they fell to the lower echelons of the League structure. However, they returned in 1981 and ended Liverpool's unbeaten home run of 85 matches.

Brighton have proved to be a thorn in the Reds' side especially in cup competitions. They met Liverpool in successive seasons: 1982/83 and 1983/84. Former player Jimmy Melia was managing the south-coast side who made it all the way to Wembley after the first meeting when another Liverpool old boy, Jimmy Case, sealed a 2–1 fifth-round win at Anfield. A year later and one round earlier only the venue changed as Brighton cruised to a 2–0 home win. Liverpool have met the Seagulls, who have experienced substantially straitened times, since and secured easy wins.

UNBEATEN RUNS

In the year of the club's acceptance to the Football League, Liverpool claimed the Second Division crown, remaining unbeaten for the entire 28-game season. That record remained unparalleled by the club for almost 100 years. The 1987/88 term saw the club equal Leeds United's achievement of remaining without a League defeat from the start of a season. 15 years earlier the Yorkshire outfit went on a 29-match streak. Alan Clarke, an integral member of Leeds' squad then, saw his younger brother halt Liverpool's attempts to claim the mark as their own. Wayne Clarke scored the only goal of that 30th game – away at Everton.

An 85-match unbeaten run at home included 65 league ties, 9 in the League Cup, 7 European matches and 6 FA Cup games. All were played between 21 January 1978 and 31 January 1981.

A DREAM SIGNING

Transfer rumours are often rife in the media. Amid the speculation it attracts in a 24-hour media culture was the story of Liverpool's interest in a French defender, Didier Baptiste, back in November 1999. As the Reds were then managed by a native of that country there may have been nothing unusual about this reported interest – at least at face value. Except that the little known under-21 international speculated about didn't play for AS Monaco as was thought, or indeed any other Ligue 1 club.

He was a character from the Sky TV football drama *Dream Team* played by a British actor credited as Tom Redhill but who was also known as Sacha Grunpeter. At the time Baptiste was being lined up for a move to fictional

Premiership team Harchester United. Fees between £1 million and £3.5 million were quoted for the left-back who during an episode of the show revealed that he would 'sign for an English club who have a French manager.' Just how this found its way into media outlets is unknown, but before the truth was out, those who published the story did at least cover their backs by suggesting Houllier would face stiff competition from Arsenal boss Arsène Wenger.

THE BOOT ROOM DYNASTY

The boot room remained an inner sanctum of several Liverpool managerial teams throughout many years. Yet the infamous piece of Anfield was little more than a cubby hole and was exactly what it sounds like: a small room with football boots covering its walls that once stood in a corridor of the Main Stand. Bill Shankly's reign is generally accepted to be the origin of what is now viewed as the Anfield tradition of the coaching staff getting together and chewing over team affairs. When a manager decided to leave there would be no conjecture as to which big name might replace him. It was generally accepted that one of the unassuming deputies would step into the breach and maintain the seamless running of a well-oiled red machine.

A select group of opposition managers may have been invited in to share a tot of whisky or two following a game, but a closed-door policy operated in respect of everyone bar the coaching staff themselves. Each and every would-be visitor, including the then manager, had to knock before gaining admittance which, in most cases, would be denied. It was pulled down during Graeme Souness's reign to accommodate expanded press room facilities. It now only exists as a byword for managerial excellence and loyalty.

TWO SHANKLYS – TWO ANFIELDS

Two men with the surname Shankly have managed British clubs – brothers Bob and Bill – and each did so at Anfield. Or at least in the former's case Annfield – home of Stirling Albion where he was in charge of team affairs for three years until joining the Beano's board. Bob Shankly previously had spells with Stenhousemuir, Falkirk, Third Lanark, Dundee and Hibernian. He led Dundee to the League title in 1962 and semi-final of the European Cup a season later. They beat AC Milan at Dens Park but went out 5–2 on aggregate. A Scottish Cup final quickly followed. At that stage he had a more impressive CV than his younger sibling. As Hibernian boss he reached a League Cup final in 1969, by which time Bill was well on the way to completing his Bastion of Invincibility.

FREE AND EASY

When the little-known Belgian footballer Jean-Marc Bosman took his contract dispute to the European Court of Justice very few people, in or outside the game, could have realised the impact the eventual decision would have. The well-documented ramifications of his complaint now ensure that any player who comes out of contract can negotiate a deal with another club and the team he is leaving being entitled to no transfer fee whatsoever. In addition, should six months or less of the player's existing contract remain, then he is then free to sign an agreement to join a foreign club once that contract has finally expired. As no transfer fee is involved, the player can negotiate a bumper pay day – his estimated value.

Steve McManaman is the biggest name to leave the club under the ruling. He joined Real Madrid in the summer of

1999. Liverpool have been careful to guard against prized assets running their contracts down since McManaman exercised his opportunity. Players leaving with such freedom of movement are only those deemed surplus to requirements.

WE'VE WON IT FIVE TIMES

Following promotion in 1962, Liverpool's second season in the top flight not only landed a first championship in 25 years, it guaranteed the club's first appearance in the European Champions Cup. The Reds had spent the best part of a decade in Division Two but on 14 September 1964 began their adventure in one of Europe's furthest outposts – against KR Reykjavík of Iceland. The trip, which started with a coach journey from Liverpool to Scotland, caused some alarm to those on the flight over. The pilot decided to give his passengers an opportunity to view one of the country's many volcanoes as it billowed smoke. However, the unannounced sight-seeing opportunity led many to believe the plane's wing was ablaze.

Reaching a semi-final against Inter Milan, one which the players believe they were cheated out of, suggested there was plenty of potential, though Liverpool's pursuit of Europe's ultimate prize failed to reach such dizzy heights until the 1976/77 season and a final with Germany's Borussia Mönchengladbach in Rome. Liverpool led at the break but were pegged back a few minutes into the second half. The Reds reclaimed the lead before wrapping matters up with a penalty 8 minutes from the end. A year later Liverpool were defending their trophy at Wembley. Bruges were charged with the job of stopping them and held their lines until a perfectly weighted pass from Graeme Souness set up Kenny Dalglish with a chance. It was a comfortable, if narrow, win.

A Kennedy double-act brought the European Cup back for a third time, in Paris three years later, when Liverpool took on Real Madrid. Ray Kennedy took a throw on the left which fell to the feet of his namesake, Alan. The full-back edged into the penalty area before unleashing a shot past Agustin.

The same player proved to be the match-winner when Liverpool next conquered Europe's finest in 1984. Another major player in that victory was Bruce Grobbelaar, the eccentric goalkeeper who had replaced Ray Clemence after that game against Real Madrid. Back at Rome's Olympic Stadium (scene of Liverpool's European Cup glory against Borussia Mönchengladbach), they faced home side AS Roma. A 1–1 draw after 90 minutes and extra time forced the sides to endure a penalty shoot-out. The kicks were taken directly in front of the Italian fans who jeered and whistled. Youngster Steve Nicol skyed the first. Later Bruno Conti missed after Grobbelaar decided to employ a bit of gamesmanship with his antics on the line. The keeper repeated his routine for the next opponent who also shot high and wide. Alan Kennedy hit a shot firmly in, sending the keeper the wrong way.

The same method decided the 2005 final after Liverpool retrieved a three-goal half-time deficit with a treble inside six minutes. Jerzy Dudek then denied Andriy Shevchenko in the shoot-out and secured victory.

I DON'T KNOW WHAT IT IS, BUT I LOVE IT

In part it seems the 1984 European Cup triumph owes much to North-East singer/songwriter Chris Rea – a rumoured Middlesbrough fan for his sins. There were, as ever, huge numbers of Liverpool fans present in Rome, but unlike the atmosphere in 1977 when red colours made up roughly three-quarters of the numbers, the vast majority of this 65,000-strong crowd were home fans. Merseyside spectators were doing their best to be heard but determined to throw the gauntlet down, Graeme Souness took in much of a pre-match walk around the pitch and warm up in front of the baying Italian hordes.

With the crowd psyched out, the opposing players were next. Showing no signs of anxiety, Liverpool lined up alongside their opponents then broke out into a chorus from Rea's recent single 'I don't know what it is, but I love it'. It was a tune that had been played frequently within the Anfield dressing room. Souness, Craig Johnston and David Hodgson led the impromptu karaoke session but were soon joined by almost a dozen throats. It was something members of the Roma side later admitted had them baffled but convinced Liverpool were without nerves ahead of kick-off.

A BADGE OF HONOUR

Aside from giving Liverpool the chance to commission a shirt that they would play the 2005/06 European campaign in (complete with five stars representing each Champions Cup win), the Miracle of Istanbul earned the Reds a chance to keep the trophy and have a UEFA badge on their jersey sleeves when playing in competitions organised by that governing body. Awarded to teams who win the trophy five times or on three successive occasions, it is a huge honour – though has one drawback. It's blue.

The trophy which now graces Anfield forever has a dent on the handle courtesy of it hitting the floor during post-match celebrations. A decision not to repair it was taken as it was felt the damage added to the character of the occasion.

Though European competition only began in the early 1950s, in earlier days, before it was formalised, Liverpool were invited to take on a succession of Italian sides after winning the title in 1922. After warming up with a defeat to Burnley, third-placed finishers in Division One, they soundly beat select XIs representing the Emilia then Liguria and Toscana regions. Pro Vercelli, their Prima Divisione counterparts who had also won back-to-back crowns, kept Liverpool to a goalless draw. Genoa were handsomely beaten before the tour finished with a 2–2 draw at Pisa.

CHAMPIONS OF EUROPE WITHOUT PLAYING A MINUTE

Only a select band of players are able to call themselves European Champions. The continent's biggest title has been won by a host of Liverpool legends, though there are others able to claim the same honour with far less celebrated careers. As up to five substitutes were allowed to be named, a number of fringe players sat on the bench. That includes some who claimed medals despite never playing a single minute for the first team. Goalkeepers Peter McDonnell and Bob Bolder are among that number from the 1977 and 1984 finals respectively. Each left Anfield with nothing more than reserve team football under their belts. McDonnell lost his gong after the game. Rumours persist that it was taken by an unnamed club official who passed it to a member of the first team, who in turn gave it to a player who had contributed to the opening rounds but missed the final.

Pegguy Arphexad had left Liverpool by 2005 when the trophy was won in Istanbul, but all seven of his career medals came as a non-playing substitute. He won the Worthington Cup with Leicester in that capacity in 2000. A year later he was back as a Liverpool player and repeated the feat. It actually was the first leg of a treble-winning campaign with the FA and UEFA Cup following. Medals in the Charity Shield and European Super Cup, plus a watching brief while Jerzy Dudek starred in the 2003 Carling Cup victory, meant he won six honours in three years at Anfield by doing little more than keeping the bench warm. He played 505 minutes of first-team football while a Liverpool player and in the 99 times he was named on the bench, got onto the pitch just once – in a 6–0 victory at Ipswich Town.

THE WAITING GAME

In an era of substitute goalkeepers it isn't unusual for stoppers to spend lengthy periods at a club without getting a game. Although Tony Warner did no more than sit on the bench a record 121 times, perhaps the unluckiest stopper in the club's history is Jorgen Nielsen who spent a month shy of 5 years on the Anfield payroll. While on the bench in September 1999 for a Merseyside derby with Everton he would normally have got a chance as Sander Westerveld was sent off during a tempestuous Anfield encounter. Francis Jeffers received his marching orders at the same time, as the two had been fighting. Unfortunately for the Norwegian, just 4 minutes earlier his manager Gerard Houllier had pitched Vladimir Šmicer on for Titi Camara – the third and final substitution he was allowed to make. It meant an outfield player had to go in goal and Steve Staunton had the gloves thrown in his direction.

THE LITTLE RED BOOK OF LIVERPOOL FC

MILESTONE GOALS – THE LEAGUE CUP

The most successful side in League Cup history, Liverpool didn't take the competition seriously for many years. However, a huge number of goals have been racked up in the tournament – 413 from 204 matches.

1	Tommy Leishman	v Luton Town	19 October 1960
100	Kenny Dalglish	v Birmingham City	2 December 1980
200	John Wark	v Fulham	23 September 1986
300	Robbie Fowler	v Crystal Palace	8 March 1995
400	Steven Gerrard	v Arsenal	9 January 2007

HE GOT AN EDUCATION
FROM THE KOP

Had he not made a commitment to manage Manchester United, Matt Busby could have taken the Anfield hotseat as he was offered the job. However, it is worth reflecting that if he had been in a position to accept or indeed been obligated to do so, his great friend Bill Shankly may never have become the Anfield manager.

Busby joined the Reds from, of all clubs considering his ultimate destination in football, Manchester City. War saw his Anfield career limited to a mere four seasons. From a first selection just days after he sealed an £8,000 transfer in March 1936, only injury robbed him of a berth in the half-back line. He acknowledged that a new scene restored his love of the game. Though well thought of at Maine Road, he had by his own admission grown a little stale, so relished the challenge. Like many Scots, he took well to the city of Liverpool.

The club captaincy was bestowed on him shortly before war broke out. It was after peace was declared that the idea of him being given a role in team affairs was first mooted; initially as a coach. If possible, Busby wanted to take charge of a club but by the time this option was debated Matt had promised his services to the Old Trafford outfit. The Reds' directors resisted United's approach but the then chairman Billy McConnell was instrumental in persuading his colleagues to let him go.

THE SECOND STRING

Until recent years, when the emphasis of reserve team football changed, Liverpool's second-string coaches have been able to call upon an impressive array of talent. It is no exaggeration to say that among the up-and-coming hopefuls there were as often as not seasoned professionals and internationals all turning out to keep not just match fit but hoping to stake their claim for a first-team place. This may be one of the reasons why the Reds have claimed an impressive 18 reserve team championships. The most concentrated spell of success came in the 1970s and 1980s during which time Roy Evans steered his squad to 8 titles in 10 years. A plaque also commemorates a hat-trick of successes from 1968 to 1971.

GOOD ENOUGH FOR HIS COUNTRY – BUT NOT THE REDS

Fierce competition within the first team may have been one reason why Liverpool's reserves were full of internationals, though some players represented their respective countries while plying their trade in the second string – many before making a debut for the Reds. Others did so without ever featuring in a first XI game.

St Mirren forward Frank McGarvey drew many comparisons with Kenny Dalglish prior to his signing for the Reds in May 1979 at a fee of £270,000. He made a Scotland debut in a Home International with Northern Ireland, mostly because of his form at Love Street. It was only a 5-minute run towards the end of the game but it emphasised the upward curve of his career. However, there was a starting berth – alongside Dalglish – for a prestige Hampden Park friendly with Argentina. His spell at Anfield lasted just 10 months. The player struggled to settle and failed to break into Bob Paisley's plans. When Celtic offered the exact amount paid out, a return north of the border was arranged.

Ian Rush was a part of Mike England's plans and won the first of his 67 Wales caps over 6 months before Bob Paisley asked him to deputise for Kenny Dalglish in a League game at Ipswich Town. Ken DeMange could not force a breakthrough but in May 1987 he made the Republic of Ireland side as a substitute in a 1–0 win over Brazil. Jim Magilton served a number of clubs making well over 500 appearances and earning 52 caps with Northern Ireland. An international debut in which he scored against Poland came less than 3 months after he left Anfield for Oxford United, but the Belfast-born midfielder was called into the senior squad for some end-of-season friendlies prior to his departure.

Javier Mascherano was at River Plate rather than beside the River Mersey when making his Argentina debut in 2003, 18 days before he had made a first-team outing for his club. His displays at youth grades were the reason for his promotion.

PLAYING THROUGH THE PAIN BARRIER

Gerry Byrne displayed he was as tough as teak throughout his Liverpool career but the 1965 FA Cup final surpassed any other show of strength as he played close to the full 90 minutes and then extra time with not only a gashed shin but a broken collarbone. Many players would have been inhibited by just one of those problems, but not Gerry. In a bid to hide the shoulder injury from a Leeds side who would have exploited it, he ignored the blinding pain and refused to have the limb in a splint or even protect it by keeping the arm close to his body. The full-back played a blinder and even sent in the cross which set up Liverpool's first goal. A few days later the European Cup semi-final first leg with Inter Milan took place at Anfield. Always looking for the psychological edge Bill Shankly sent Byrne out, sling draped around his neck, along with another injury victim Gordon Milne, who had missed out at Wembley. The two paraded the FA Cup in front of the Kop. The noise level shot through the roof and played no small part in Liverpool's infamous 3–1 win. Those heroics proved not to be a one-off. A year later in a Cup Winners' Cup tie against Celtic, Byrne dislocated an elbow. The club doctor twisted it back into position and he carried on. Little wonder Shanks described him as the toughest player he had ever seen.

THIS IS YOUR CAPTAIN SPEAKING

The first captain of Liverpool Football Club was former Evertonian Andrew Hannah. He had been an important member of the old Everton and was brought back to Anfield by John Houlding after the rebels had moved out and the new club formed. Other skippers from Liverpool's early days include Alex Raisbeck, who steered the Reds to their first two League Championships in 1901 and 1906. With Harry Lowe injured, Bob Ferguson became the first man to lead Liverpool out in an FA Cup final in 1914. During the 1920s Walter Wadsworth, Eph Longworth and Don McKinlay all captained the team.

Although not a definitive list of each player to have skippered the Reds when the club captain has been missing through injury or suspension, all the club's official post-war leaders are listed below:

Willie Fagan	1946–7
Phil Taylor	1947–53
Bill Jones	1953–4
Billy Liddell	1954–5
Ronnie Moran	1955–60
Dick White	1960–1
Ron Yeats	1961–70
Tommy Smith	1970–3
Emlyn Hughes	1973–9
Phil Thompson	1979–82
Graeme Souness	1982–4
Phil Neal	1984–5
Alan Hansen	1985–8
Ronnie Whelan	1988–91
Mark Wright	1991–2
Ian Rush	1992–6
John Barnes	1996–7
Paul Ince	1997–9
Jamie Redknapp	1999–2002
Sami Hyypia	2002–3
Steven Gerrard	2003– present

Though the tradition is that captains lift any silverware won, before his retirement in 1983 the Liverpool players who beat Manchester United to the Milk Cup insisted Bob Paisley go up the Wembley steps to pick up the trophy. It is a tradition that has come back in recent times. Vice-captain Robbie Fowler accepted the Worthington Cup in 2001 but injured club skipper Jamie Redknapp was ushered forward to hoist the FA Cup aloft along with Fowler at the same venue two months later. Fowler had started on the bench for the game, the same position he occupied when the UEFA Cup final kicked off four days later. By the end of the game he had been introduced and invited Sami Hyypia, who had been given the captain's armband at the start, to receive the trophy.

NO CHARITY SHOWN

As regular winners of the domestic game's two top honours, the League and FA Cup, Liverpool have played in a fair few of what are now pre-season curtain-raisers. The first appearance came just four days after the end of the 1921/22 season. As League Champions Liverpool took on FA Cup holders Huddersfield Town, the Terriers taking the honours with a single goal. That match was played at Old Trafford but Liverpool's first Charity Shield showpiece at Wembley was a tempestuous affair with Leeds United. Kevin Keegan and Billy Bremner were sent off as tempers boiled over. Keegan threw his shirt to the ground in disgust and frustration at his dismissal. Liverpool eventually triumphed 6–5 on penalties following a 1–1 draw after 90 minutes.

Until the opening of the 2010/11 season Liverpool had played in 20 Charity Shield games winning 10, losing 5 and sharing the silverware on 5 occasions.

APPEARANCES

Ian Callaghan's 857 Liverpool games is a tally which will take some beating. In fact, post-Bosman and with freedom of contract, there is some likelihood that it will never be bettered as 15 seasons of consistency is the benchmark any player would need to meet. The top ten appearance makers for the club in all games are:

1	Ian Callaghan	857 (7)
2	Ray Clemence	665
3	Emlyn Hughes	665
4	Ian Rush	660 (30)
5	Phil Neal	650 (2)
6	Tommy Smith	638 (1)
7	Jamie Carragher	630 (21)
8	Bruce Grobbelaar	628
9	Alan Hansen	620 (2)
10	Chris Lawler	549

Appearances as a substitute in brackets.

A MICKEY MOUSE GAME

Friendlies in aid of charity or benevolence to individuals have been commonplace to Liverpool Football Club. Virtually since its inception the team drew a crowd and played their first testimonial in March 1893 against Bootle Boys' Brigade in aid of David Kirkwood. Some 110 years later, in June 2003, Fleetwood Town earned a prestige friendly with Liverpool when youngster Dominic Hoyle found himself sat next to Gerard Houllier on a flight back from his holiday at EuroDisney.

The two talked football throughout the journey and when Fleetwood owner Mick Hoyle, father of the 8-year-old, grabbed a chance at the end of the journey he asked if a game could be scheduled against the North-West Counties League side. One was swiftly arranged. In fact it had to be switched from the Highbury Road ground in the fishing port to Blackpool's much larger Bloomfield Road to accommodate the numbers as a strong team was promised.

A DIVIDE RARELY CROSSED

Although he enjoyed a less than average stay with Liverpool embracing a mere handful of first-team games, Phil Chisnall has a particular claim to fame. The forward is the last player to be directly transferred between Old Trafford and Anfield. He left Manchester United in April 1964 for £25,000, making 9 appearances over 3 seasons before accepting a move to Southend United.

Liverpool and Manchester United have competed for the same signatures and coveted a number of each other's players over the near half-century which has intervened. However, despite some close relations at boardroom level, transfers have never been discussed – at least not in a developed nature. The closest any player has come to crossing the East Lancs divide is Rafael Benitez's attempt to land Gabriel Heinze after the Argentine was told he could leave Old Trafford in the summer of 2007 should United's valuation be met. The Reds made a £6.8 million bid which was the sum Sir Alex Ferguson stipulated, but the Scot vetoed the offer stating that any transfer was conditional on a move abroad or to a club who were not a direct rival for honours. The left-back, who had begged to be given an opportunity at Anfield, joined Real Madrid – £8 million changing hands.

There are a few players who have turned out for both sides using other clubs as a buffer between stints at Anfield or Old Trafford. However, that only Peter Beardsley, Paul Ince and Michael Owen are among their number may indicate the intense rivalry generated by the clubs.

THE TURKEY CAN WAIT

These days players are allowed to spend the majority of Christmas Day with their families; with such a busy festive period it is seen as the right thing to do. However, it wasn't always this way. Up until 1958 and with very few exceptions, players up and down the country would be expected to turn out. Liverpool's last fixture on that date involved a long trek to Grimsby – the Reds lost 3–1. Liverpool's last goal on Christmas Day came courtesy of Tony Rowley, a season ticket holder after he finished playing, who scored 38 goals in his 61 appearances for the club.

HAPPY GOAL RETURNS

Although it is difficult to trace birth dates for some of those who played for the club prior to the Second World War there are 17 known occasions when Liverpool players have scored a goal on the same day they are blowing out the candles on their cakes. Only Terry McDermott has managed to achieve the feat twice. The list is as follows:

Tom Bromilow	7 October 1922	v Everton
Gordon Hodgson (2)	16 April 1927	v Bury
Robert Done	27 April 1929	v Blackburn Rovers
Alf Hanson	27 February 1937	v Brentford

Berry Nieuwenhuys	5 November 1938	v Portsmouth
Billy Liddell	10 January 1948	v Nottingham Forest
John Evans	28 August 1954	v Derby County
Jimmy Melia	1 November 1958	v Stoke
Steve Heighway	25 November 1972	v Tottenham Hotspur
Phil Thompson	21 January 1978	v Birmingham City
Terry McDermott	8 December 1979	v Aston Villa
Terry McDermott	8 December 1981	v Arsenal
Ronnie Whelan (2)	25 September 1982	v Southampton
Phil Neal	20 February 1985	v York City
Steve McManaman	11 February 1992	v Bristol Rovers
David Burrows	25 October 1992	v Norwich City
Robbie Fowler	9 April 2006	v Bolton Wanderers
Peter Crouch	30 January 2007	v West Ham United

THE TEAM PLAYING IN BLUE AND WHITE IS LIVERPOOL

Liverpool may be universally known as the Reds but this hasn't been the only colour the team has played in. Over their formative years the club turned out in blue and white quarters. Red only became the 'home colours' a couple of seasons on. White shorts remained until 1964 when Bill Shankly decided the players looked far more formidable in all red. He used Ron Yeats as proof and it seems he had a point. The first game Liverpool played top to toe in red was against Anderlecht in the 1964/65 European Cup. The Belgians crashed out 4–0 on aggregate after a 3–0 win at Anfield was followed by a single-goal victory in the return leg. The solid red shirts remained until 1982 at which time a fine vertical pinstripe was introduced. A return to plain designs coincided with a change of kit manufacturer. Although the trimmings, shades and other small details regularly undergo slight alterations, it wasn't until the early 1990s that stripes, this time far wider and running diagonally across the rib area, adulterated the pure red.

Away colours have been extremely varied. Until the 1980s it was usually white – either all white or with black shorts. It transformed later into yellow with a red trim. For a single season during the decade it reverted to white shirts with black shorts. Then yellow returned once more. Since 1987 a whole host of colours have been used to avoid clashes. These include various combinations of silver, green, black, gold and ecru.

FLAGGING UP A NEW KIT

All manner of items were in short supply after the Second World War. Rationing, which ensured supplies of many items remained available during the years of post-conflict austerity, carried on almost a decade after the Nazis were defeated. It led to a very early version of recycling which included clothing. Football clubs were not untouched, with shirts worn until they were fit to drop off a player's back – patched, darned and stitching mended. It must have seemed like manna from heaven when Liverpool were given a set of freshly tailored jerseys by troops they were due to entertain in matches against servicemen.

The games were aimed at raising morale and took place in the now free Germany at stadiums in Celle and Hanover just weeks after the war ended. Whether the origin of the shirts was declared to the club is unknown, but they were assembled from flags which had once adorned every part of the Third Reich until they were pulled down once Hitler fell. It is speculated that the same jerseys were used throughout the first post-war season – when Liverpool won a fifth League Championship.

OUR BREAD AND BUTTER

Although the championship crown hasn't been to Anfield since 1990, there is very little doubt that the club's trophy cabinet is where every Liverpool fan would like to see it return. Regardless of any particular guise it may hide under, to finish top of your country's leading division is the ultimate prize.

As Bill Shankly once said, 'It's our bread and butter.'

The Premiership is still to be won by the Reds but before its inception in 1992 Liverpool had been crowned champions 18 times. It was a record light years ahead of every other club at the time and one it took Manchester United 16 years to reel in and level up.

MY TEAM? IT'S THE SAME AS LAST SEASON

Consistency is a Liverpool watchword which has formed one of the many bases for the Reds' phenomenal successes. Injury and suspension will very often limit the availability of squad members but in the 1965/66 championship campaign Bill Shankly used a mere 14 players over the course of the 42-game League programme. This prompted him to simply announce that he would be fielding the same team as last year when enquiries over his line-ups were made. Only Geoff Strong with 21 games and 1 as a substitute, Alf Arrowsmith with 3 appearances plus 2 calls from the bench and Bobby Graham with a single run out in the last game of the season, missed more than 5 games.

The only other man to get a look in during the cup campaigns was Phil Chisnall who started the first leg of the European Cup Winners' Cup semi-final with Celtic at Parkhead. The club played 52 games overall.

MILESTONE GOALS – THE FA CUP

Liverpool have scored 670 goals from 404 FA Cup games. The landmark strikes are below:

1	Tom Wyllie	v Nantwich	15 October 1892
100	Arthur Goddard	v Gainsborough Trinity	14 January 1911
200	Syd Roberts	v Yeovil	12 January 1935
300	Roger Hunt	v Wrexham	9 January 1963
400	Steve Heighway	v Carlisle United	29 January 1977
500	Craig Johnston	v Manchester City	13 March 1988
600	Jamie Redknapp	v Coventry City	3 January 1998

BATTLES OF BRITAIN

Liverpool have met sides from the British Isles in European competition on 16 occasions and so far have a better than average record.

Year	Competition	Opposition	Agg Score
1964/65	Cup Winners' Cup	Celtic	2–1
1970/71	Fairs Cup	Hibernian	3–0
1970/71	Fairs Cup	Leeds United	0–1

Year	Competition	Opposition	Agg Score
1972/73	UEFA Cup	Tottenham Hotspur	2–2
		(won on away goals)	
1975/76	UEFA Cup	Hibernian	3–2
1976/77	European Cup	Crusaders	7–0
1978/79	European Cup	Nottingham Forest	0–2
1980/81	European Cup	Aberdeen	5–0
1997/98	UEFA Cup	Celtic	2–2
		(won on away goals)	
2002/03	UEFA Cup	Celtic	1–3
2004/05	Champions League	Chelsea	1–0
2005/06	Champions League Qualifiers	TNS	6–0
2006/07	Champions League	Chelsea	1–1
		(won 4–1 on penalties)	
2007/08	Champions League	Arsenal	5–3
2007/08	Champions League	Chelsea	3–4
2008/09	Champions League	Chelsea	5–7

CROSSING THE PARK

There have been a relatively large number of deals between Liverpool and Everton. Almost 30 over the past century may not seem many, but it makes the Reds and Blues among the most prolific traders in domestic football. Some have had spells as youth players at one or the other club before swapping sides, but a number have involved transfer fees. The first player to make the short trip across Stanley Park was Fred Geary who left Goodison for Liverpool in 1897. Everton's first recruit from their neighbours was Dick Forshaw in 1926.

Until the year 2000 Liverpool hadn't made a purchase from Goodison Park since 1959. Dave Hickson, a tall and well-built striker, was a hero to thousands of Evertonians and his move created a shock Liverpudlians can probably only understand by imagining Steven Gerrard or Fernando Torres signing for Everton. Over 20 years passed before the next piece of cheque book activity as the Blues themselves oversaw a moratorium of 21 years between 1961 and 1982. David Johnson, who started his career at Everton as an apprentice but came to Liverpool via Ipswich Town, went back to Goodison after suffering from Ian Rush's gradual emergence. Howard Kendall signed him for £100,000 but when his second spell lasted just 37 games it became clear Liverpool had enjoyed the best Johnson had to offer. Johnson, along with Peter Beardsley, are the only players to score for both clubs in Merseyside derbies.

A HEAVY DEFEAT

The club's record league defeat came against Birmingham City in Division Two on 11 December 1954. Billy Liddell scored after 16 minutes in the calamitous 9–1 defeat at St Andrews.

ALE HOUSE FOOTBALL

Alongside his duties as a Liverpool player, Phil Thompson managed his local pub's side – the Falcon, a drinking establishment in Kirkby. In a style very typical of his mentor, Bill Shankly, he named the outfit as his second team when asked about other football allegiances for magazine profiles. During the 1980/81 season he had been ticked-off after the League Cup was left on the bus which took the side through the city's streets, though it was eventually returned to the club by the depot manager. On being told that ultimate responsibility for looking after trophies fell in his lap as captain, even if that meant taking silverware home, he proudly took the European Cup to his favoured watering hole bringing it over in the boot of his Capri. After photographs were taken with fans and the silverware passed between many hands it was taken back to Anfield for a photocall with the nation's press.

GOAL MISERS

Liverpool's best defensive record over the course of a season came in the 1978/79 campaign. Over 42 games, a defence crammed with names which would make any forward line shudder, let a paltry 16 goals past them. This comprised just 12 away from home and a miserly 4 at Anfield. Liverpool won the championship that season which may go some way to proving that a good backline is the cornerstone of a winning team. Certainly Messrs Neal, Clemence, Kennedy, Thompson, Hansen and Hughes can claim to have been a huge factor in that triumph. On just one occasion did any team score more than once against them in a game – when Aston Villa beat the Reds 3–1 at Villa Park.

In 1990/91 Arsenal powered to the championship conceding just 18 goals over a 38-game campaign. Liverpool had 18 goals recorded against them in winning the 1893/94 Second Division crown. The club were also unbeaten, although that was over an extremely truncated season, comprising just 28 games. Liverpool's next best mark over a 42-game term came on three separate occasions when 24 goals were conceded in the 1968/69, 1970/71 and 1987/88 seasons.

DERBY DELIGHTS

Without doubt the most intense and eagerly fought rivalry in club football is the Merseyside derby. The initial clash between the city's two teams took place on 13 October 1894 at Goodison Park. Everton took first blood cruising to a 3–0 victory. Anfield staged its first encounter just over a month later which finished 2–2 after Jimmy Ross equalised with a penalty in the dying minutes.

All League matches between the clubs have taken place in England's top division. Up until the end of the 2009/10 season, the Mersey giants had taken each other on 213 times in first-class competitions.

The breakdown in each competition is as follows:

	P	W	D	L	F	A
Football/ Premier League	182	70	56	56	247	214
FA Cup	22	9	6	7	35	26
League Cup	4	2	1	1	2	1
Others	5	3	1	1	9	4
	213	84	64	65	293	245

Liverpool have the best record in the overall head-to-head. They have also made Everton endure the longest winless streak in the fixture – 15 matches from March 1972 to April 1978. The two clubs had six meetings during the 1986/87 season, though technically a couple in the two-legged final of the Screen Sports Super Cup were held over from the previous campaign. Liverpool remained unbeaten with 4 wins and a couple of draws.

Reds fans have had plenty of opportunity to crow about their superiority, but never more so than when enjoying big wins, of which there have been plenty. As early as 1922 a capacity crowd saw Liverpool run out 5–1 home winners.

Anfield played host to another 6-goal encounter 13 years later, only this time Liverpool scored them all. Fred Howe proved to be the hero of the day, bagging 4. Legendary marksman and scourge of all Evertonians, Ian Rush, notched the same amount in the devastating 5–0 victory at Goodison Park in November 1982, which is the Reds' best away win in derby history.

In terms of high scoring by both sides, the greatest aggregate score in a game came during February 1933. Harold Barton scored a hat-trick in Liverpool's 7–4 home win. The FA Cup fifth-round tie between the clubs in 1967 was witnessed by over 100,000 fans of both clubs. 64,851 crammed in to Goodison to watch the home side squeeze through by a single goal. Across Stanley Park 40,149 watched events unfold on television screens.

MERSEYSIDE'S OTHER CLUB

A League meeting with Tranmere Rovers, the team often referred to as 'Merseyside's other club', has yet to take place. Even the cup competitions have only managed to pair the sides together on a couple of occasions, the first being a fourth-round FA Cup tie in February 1934. Though Tranmere, then of the Third Division North, were drawn at home, they agreed to switch the game to Anfield and were beaten 3–1. In the three meetings since that game, the Prenton Park outfit have managed just a single draw – a goalless encounter in a League Cup tie in August 1979. Liverpool won the replay 4–0 and a victory almost as resounding was handed out when the pair were drawn in the quarter-finals of the 2000/01 FA Cup competition. The Reds came through 4–2 and went on to lift the trophy.

31 meetings have taken place in friendlies, testimonials and wartime games, as well as the Birkenhead Hospitals Cup. Tranmere have won eight of these games, the most remarkable being a 6–5 victory in a fundraiser for Rovers' long-serving full-back Ray Mathias in April 1976. Ray Clemence netted a hat-trick including two strikes from the penalty spot.

THE OTHER MERSEYBEAT

Away from football, Liverpool was becoming the centre of a cultural phenomenon in the 1960s; The Beatles and others from the Merseybeat scene were sweeping across the world. Liverpool, a place many abroad had only heard of in terms of its history as a shipping port, was suddenly the most talked-about city on the globe.

In October 1963 Gerry and the Pacemakers took a song from Rodgers and Hammerstein's musical *Carousel* to number one, replacing Essex band the Tremeloes. 'You'll Never Walk Alone' was a low-key part of the second act used to comfort and encourage a character whose husband is killed during a failed robbery. The song is repeated in the final scene during a high school graduation class of which the dead man's daughter is a member. Originally recorded in 1945, it had been released by eight other artists prior to Gerry and the Pacemakers, including Frank Sinatra, but had never topped the British hit parade until that four-week stint.

There was a certain pride about those local bands who had done so well in the music world, and just like any other popular tune during the decade, it was played and sung along to. When the recording started to drop from the top spot it was taken away from the playlist, but the fans continued to sing it and were so fervent about the track that a letter-writing campaign to the club and *Liverpool Echo* was mounted. It was quickly reinstated – only missing a single week – and has remained on the turntable from then on.

THE ENEMY WITHIN

It may seem hard to believe that any Liverpool player would want to lose a game with Manchester United, but that is precisely what four Anfield players were found guilty of in 1915. Rumours that the Football League were about to suspend the professional game due to the advent of a war between various powers in central Europe were rife. Although nobody knew exactly how long the conflict would last, and projections were that it could well only rage until Christmas, players justifiably worried that it would be long enough to end their careers. Some knew it would, as no matter if the war lasted six months or six years, their playing days were over and the temptation to make as much money as they could before it happened proved too much for some. Liverpool were safe in mid-table while United languished far too close to its foot for comfort. They would host the game and if both points were claimed it would only aid their fight against relegation. Of course if the result of a game was already decided prior to a ball being kicked there was the chance for those in the know to make an awful lot of money by well-placed betting.

United had 7-1 odds to win 2–0 and the game played on Good Friday brought nothing but suspicion on itself. George Anderson put United ahead and was expected to double the advantage when a penalty was awarded in the home side's favour. He was the regular penalty-taker and had a good record from the spot. However, Patrick O'Connell took responsibility and blazed his shot well wide. Irregular enough. But when Liverpool striker Fred Pagnam hit the bar he was openly remonstrated for the effort. Anderson grabbed a second late in the game. Bookmakers decided that a fix had been arranged and offered a reward for information leading to the identification of those involved in the planning. An inquiry was set up and after lengthy consideration agreed that a betting coup had taken place. Four players from each club were held to be responsible and were immediately banned for life – though these sentences were revoked in all but one case as a reward for sterling service on behalf of King and country.

As a former United player, Jackie Sheldon was thought to have been heavily influential. The other Anfield players named were Tommy Miller, Bob Purcell and Tom Fairfoul. The club itself was fined £250. The latter offender never returned to Liverpool while Sheldon and Miller went on to make many more appearances for the club. When he eventually left Anfield, Miller joined United.

LIVERPOOL ARGUE THE CASE FOR CHELSEA AND ARSENAL

Though the game was proved a fix, Chelsea, who had finished 19th and by virtue of that taken United's place in the drop zone, were not relegated when the Football League resumed. They were instead re-elected to the newly expanded First Division which increased from 20 to 22 teams. Possibly due to his club's involvement in the skulduggery, Liverpool chairman John McKenna gave an impassioned speech supporting the Pensioners at the League's 1919 AGM. He also suggested that Arsenal, who had occupied fifth place in Division Two, should join the elite along with the promoted sides Derby County and Preston North End in order to recognise their service as a League club. McKenna successfully suggested they replace the 20th-placed side when the 1914/15 campaign closed – none other than Tottenham Hotspur.

WAR GAMES

Though the Football League ran for a season during the First World War, the inevitable suspension of the professional game took place soon after that betting scandal. The structures were replaced by a number of specially constructed regional competitions. From September 1915 to April 1919 the Reds participated in two; the Lancashire Section Principal and Supplementary Tournaments. Liverpool claimed the Principal Championship in 1917 and the Supplementary version in successive seasons: 1917/18 and 1918/19.

The advent of the Second World War was a totally different matter. The possible repercussions of an all-out conflict with Hitler's Germany were plain for all to see. It meant the 1939/40 campaign was just three games old when abandoned. Local divisions were set up once more, but unlike those established during the previous hostilities, allowed many changes to both the rules of the game and personnel to ensure government guidelines on travel, crowding and air raids were satisfied. Guesting, a system which allowed players to turn out for teams close to their military postings, was introduced. It allowed a number of greats from other clubs to turn out for the Reds including Cliff Britton, Sam Bartram, Stan Cullis and Tom Finney. One of Finney's Preston North End team-mates, a certain

William Shankly, made his one and only appearance in a Liverpool shirt helping the Reds beat Everton 4–1 at Anfield on 30 May 1942.

In as much as these things matter, Liverpool finished top of the Football League North's Second Period which ran from December 1942 to May 1943.

FOR KING AND COUNTRY

Footballers' Battalions were formed in the First World War with players from a host of clubs battling alongside each other. Many from the same towns, cities and workplaces were sent to fight together in regiments known as Pals' Battalions. Liverpool Football Club were no different.

The Reds sent 76 men to battle Hitler in the Second World War, a figure only exceeded by Crystal Palace (98) and Wolverhampton Wanderers (91). As was the case for many clubs, the Anfield players enlisted together. Tom Cooper, a full-back who also represented England, was the only Liverpool player to die during active service when his army motorcycle collided with a bus.

THE FIRST MERSEYSIDE DERBY

Neither Anfield nor Goodison Park hosted the first clash between Liverpool and Everton. That honour went to Bootle FC's Hawthorne Road ground which was selected to host the 1893 Liverpool Senior Cup final on Saturday 22 April that year.

The cup committee had actually been at pains to keep the clubs apart in the early rounds, but both progressed unhindered with an inevitable conclusion. There was a hint of controversy about the tie. Unlike the present day where the competition is contested by reserves, both clubs usually fielded full-strength sides, but for some reason Everton arranged a match with Renton on the same day. Many observers reckoned the Blues, who had finished third in Division One, didn't fancy risking their reputation against a newly formed team outside the Football League so fielded a scratch XI while the regular first team would play in the friendly.

10,000 spectators saw Liverpool run out 1–0 winners courtesy of a Tom Wyllie strike. As may befit the antagonistic circumstances of the split which provided the city with two clubs, events on the field were not without controversy. Liverpool had a goal disallowed and Everton were denied a seemingly straightforward penalty for hand ball in the final throes of the game. Winners' medals provided and minted by Bovril were the rewards for each player, but the trophy could not be presented in the usual manner at the end of the game.

Well before they had calls for a spot kick waived away, Everton players had vehemently protested against a number of decisions by the official, Herbie Arthur. In order to ensure there would be no chance of unrest, the ceremonies were abandoned and only handed over at the beginning of the following season when Liverpool were looking to embark on their first ever campaign in the Football League. Everton issued letters of complaint about the referee, which the county FA rejected, instead issuing the Goodison side with a warning about their conduct.

DRIVING RAIN AND COLD SNAPS

By far the most notorious game to be abandoned due to adverse weather conditions was the visit of Borussia

Mönchengladbach to Anfield for the first leg of the 1972/73 UEFA Cup final. The game was called off after half an hour after torrential rain hit Merseyside. During the play which had been possible, Bill Shankly detected that the German side looked vulnerable in the air. Brian Hall had initially been selected but when the rescheduled game took place 24 hours later the 5ft 6in Hall was relegated to the substitutes' bench, taking the seat vacated by John Toshack who had a 7in height advantage over the man he replaced. Tosh's aerial threat was never underestimated by the canny Scot and it proved a sound decision as even though the towering Welshman failed to score, his very presence had the desired effect. Liverpool won 3–0, eventually lifting the trophy 3–2 on aggregate.

Not too long before Christmas 1966, a confident Liverpool set about taming Dutch champions Ajax in the European Cup. The weather in Amsterdam was atrocious. Fog restricted visibility to little more than 50 yards. FIFA rules that the referee should be able to see both ends of the pitch were disregarded after officials from the home side persuaded the man in black he only needed to see each end from the centre circle. The match was near farcical. Liverpool lost 5–1 and at one stage Shankly roamed around the pitch to gee up his players and ask what the score was. Nobody apart from those around the men he spoke to saw him.

Luton Town gained a notorious reputation with many Liverpool fans during the 1980s, particularly in January 1987. As FA Cup holders the Reds were expected to do well against Luton at the first hurdle of their defence, despite the Hatters being a fellow top-flight team. When the first game ended 0–0 an Anfield replay was scheduled to take place a few days later. Crowds had already gathered for the game when news spread about its postponement. Although cold, the Merseyside skies were virtually clear. The same could not be said for the south of England and the Luton party were snowed in at Stansted airport; as a consequence their late afternoon flight was cancelled. When the game actually took place the Reds threw everything at the visitors who managed to hold on thanks to the woodwork, a handful of good saves, dubious use of the offside flag and sheer luck. The referee tossed a coin to decide which club would host the second replay. Luton called correctly and a 3–0 victory put them through to the next stage.

NO LOVE LOST ON VALENTINE'S DAY

The record for the highest number of players sent off in a Football League match involving Liverpool is three. It was set perhaps ironically on Valentine's Day 1925 when the Reds played host to Newcastle United. Jock McNab and Walter Wadsworth were sent off for the home side, while Tommy Urwin was issued with marching orders for the visitors. The dismissals came within minutes of each other and Wadsworth's was for punching after the Newcastle man had hurled mud at him. While Wadsworth and McNab sat in the bowels of the dressing room, a knock came at the door. McNab asked who it was to be informed that it was a club director. 'Bloody hell, has the ref started to send the directors off now?' the Lanarkshire man was reported to have said.

There is confusion around exactly how many players have received their marching orders since the club was formed as records are incomplete, but Steven Gerrard currently holds the record for the most dismissals with five.

TOUCH WOOD

Footballers are guided by all manner of superstitions from lucky pants, goal-rich boots and pre-match preparation. One of the most intriguing is the troll Bob Paisley kept on his desk for many years. The mascot was sent by a well-meaning Norwegian fan and as its arrival coincided with some good results, it stayed until the manager decided to call it a day in 1983. Whether the item had any effect on team matters is debatable, but League titles, four League Cups and three European Champions Cups, not to mention all manner of minor trophies – many won after the charm was received – could point to there being something in it.

PLAYING TO THE WHISTLE

Billy Liddell scored one of the most talked-about goals that never was in a replayed fifth-round FA Cup tie with Manchester City at Anfield in February 1956. City led 2–1 with seconds remaining when Liddell gained possession on the halfway line before bursting down the flank. Checking inside, he unleashed a fierce shot past Bert Trautmann. The ball had crashed in only for the referee to rule that he had already blown his whistle. However, for sheer quantity it would be hard to beat the day Liverpool had six goals disallowed in the same game. The tally is still a League record and came during a 1–0 defeat to Blackburn Rovers at Ewood Park on 5 September 1896. The game was officiated by a Mr C.E. Sutcliffe.

DIVINE REDS

James Jackson was not your average footballer, at least not when a scratch was made below the surface of his achievements. Signed from Aberdeen during the latter months of 1925, in just under three years he was appointed club captain. His determination to follow a religious career was well known. While still playing, he became a church elder and after studying for a degree in Philosophy and Greek he undertook the necessary Theology course which would allow him to become a reverend. Liverpool fans had affectionately called him 'The Parson' for many years. He finally retired from the game in 1933, at which time he was ordained. In 1947 he conducted the funeral of former club chairman W.H. O'Connell.

Pope John Paul II, a handy goalkeeper before his ordination in 1946, was said to have had a soft spot for Liverpool. This was something which Jerzy Dudek gathered evidence in support of after a visit to the Vatican during 2004. 'I spoke to a couple of guys who are very close to the Pope,' he said, 'and they told me he is always watching our games and he is always thinking of me when Liverpool play.'

A DRINKING CUP

Like a number of top-flight clubs, Liverpool believed they had far bigger fish to fry and for most of the League Cup's early history refused to take it seriously. They actually failed to enter for a number of seasons. It was an inauspicious start to a relationship with a trophy the Reds eventually grew to love. It wasn't until 1978 that the club first reached a final and suffered a controversial replay defeat by Nottingham Forest. Three years later Liverpool were back in the final, which again went to a second game – this time at Villa Park. West Ham United had showed plucky resolve in the first meeting, equalising in the final with a late penalty. Paul Goddard put the Londoners ahead early in the replay but goals from Kenny Dalglish and Alan Hansen cancelled that advantage out. They also started an unprecedented run of success in the competition as the Reds went on to defend the trophy for a further three seasons.

In each of those years, the competition was sponsored by a government agency – the Milk Marketing Board. To assist the push that more people drink the dairy product, it became known as the Milk Cup. Tottenham Hotspur, Manchester United and Everton were the teams beaten when the trophy was under this guise.

Sponsorship has remained in place ever since, but the Reds have only ever won it subsequently when a drinks manufacturer has offered backing. Victory in the 1987 final against Arsenal was cruelly denied while Littlewoods, a Liverpool company, were putting their name to the trophy. When Liverpool next reached the final in 1995, Coca-Cola had taken over and Bolton were beaten 2–1 at Wembley Stadium. As if to signify the shift of time from those formative years as winners to the point at which a sixth cup was won, brewers Worthington were in place as backers at the time Birmingham City were beaten on penalties. Carling had entered an agreement when Liverpool beat Manchester United for a second time in the final, just two years on, in 2003.

PUTTING THEIR SHIRTS ON LIVERPOOL

Although shirt sponsorship wasn't a new invention (non-league Kettering Town had exploited the revenue-raising ability as early as January 1976), Liverpool were the first professional club to have a company name emblazoned on their strip. That came in 1979 through Japanese electronic giants Hitachi. The deal signed in July of that year saw red shirts carrying advertising when Bolton visited Anfield just weeks later.

When that agreement ended early in the next decade Crown Paints, a little closer to home in Darwen, took over the rights until the end of the 1987/88 season. They in turn were replaced by Italian firm Candy who manufactured all manner of domestic electrical appliances and backed the Reds until 1992. Both these sponsors saw their company names say goodbye in FA Cup finals. Candy remained a match-day backer for many seasons, but their replacements, Carlsberg, who will end their 18-year shirt deal in 2010, made a Wembley debut in a Charity Shield match with Leeds United. The longest-running association with any club at the time of termination, it took global financial concern Standard Chartered Bank £20 million a season to take over for at least four years.

There have been occasions over the past 31 years when a sponsor's name has not appeared on Liverpool shirts. This has usually been for European ties and friendly fixtures in countries such as Norway and France where the advertising of alcohol is illegal. The club and Carlsberg have often circumvented this by replacing it with 'Probably . . .' which refers to the well-known catchphrase the Danish brewers have exploited for decades. Quite literally a word from our sponsors.

Finnish outfit Kuusysi Lahti who played Liverpool in the first round of the 1991/92 UEFA Cup played before the world famous Kop with the name of the stand on their jerseys. However, it wasn't in tribute the terrace. Their sponsors were Kansallis-Osake-Pankki – a Finnish commercial bank who quite understandably went by the acronym KOP.

PAISLEY TIES

Until the day he left office in 1983, Bob Paisley insisted he was always a reluctant manager who initially only took the Anfield hotseat on a temporary basis as he was convinced the club would persuade Bill Shankly to return. He ended a nine-year stint at the helm as English football's most successful club boss. However, if he had his way, Bob would not have been in a position to take the post in 1974. On hanging up his boots twenty years earlier, he had intended to leave Liverpool and set himself up in business as a fruit and veg man!

A FIXTURE IN THE SIDE

The record number of ever-presents in a League season is five. This has happened in three separate seasons. Gerry Byrne, Ian Callaghan, Tommy Lawrence, Tommy Smith and Ron Yeats featured in every game of the 1965/66 campaign. Of these five only Gerry Byrne missed so much as one of the 15 cup ties also played that term. In 1968/69 Tommy Lawrence, Chris Lawler, Tommy Smith, Ian Callaghan and Peter Thompson were the only players to make it on to every team sheet. All bar Tommy Lawrence made it through the nine cup games. The last squad to equal that record was the 1983/84 championship winners. Bruce Grobbelaar, Alan Kennedy, Mark Lawrenson, Alan Hansen and Sammy Lee certainly played their part in that glory and the capture of an historic, if strength-sapping, League, European and

League Cup treble which added another 24 games to the programme. Of these only Mark Lawrenson missed out on completing all 66 games.

HAVEN'T YOU GOT A HOME TO GO TO?

The individual accolade for the most ever-present seasons during a Liverpool career belongs to Phil Neal. Of his 11½ seasons with the club, 9 were 100 per cent fulfilled. Amazingly, 8 of these campaigns came in successive seasons from 1975/76 to 1982/83.

HAT-TRICKS

Football folklore suggests that the term hat-trick derives from bygone days when fans would share an omnibus or tram to the ground along with those players they were heading off to watch, and place coins in the cap or hat of a forward. These payments were intended as an incentive to find the net three times. Those who came up with the goods were said to have performed a hat-trick.

There is no information as to whether any transport which trundled down Walton Breck Road was ridden by John Miller on the morning of 15 October 1892, and if so, how much may have been considered enough for the forward to make good any pledges he received. No doubt the funds would have been very welcome as he may well have been buying drinks for team-mates after grabbing a treble in Liverpool's first ever FA Cup game, a 4–0 win over Nantwich. Dumbarton-born Miller was the very embodiment of the nineteenth-century professional and as a free-scoring striker, could name his price. A week after that hat-trick feat he was at it again, recording another treble in a 5–0 demolition of Higher Walton. On 3 December he notched 5 more against Fleetwood Rangers.

Despite being the nephew of two Everton players, Jack Balmer is one of the most celebrated names ever to wear a red shirt. He was an amateur at Goodison Park but moved to Liverpool in 1935, staying until 1952. His greatest hour has to be scoring three consecutive hat-tricks in League games. No other Liverpool player scored during the 3–0 victory over Portsmouth, a 4–1 win against Derby County and a thrilling encounter with Arsenal which ended 4–2.

Hat-tricks on debut have been very small in number. Antonio Rowley was never a first-team regular but staked a good claim for a starting berth in the opening game of the 1954/55 season. He bagged 3 in just under half an hour including 2 in the last 4 minutes as Liverpool pipped Doncaster Rovers 3–2.

The fastest hat-trick scored by any Liverpool player came in 4 minutes and 33 seconds when Robbie Fowler's quick-fire treble demolished Arsenal at Anfield in August 1994. It remains the fastest in Premiership history.

SPORT OF KINGS (AND QUEENS)

The first royal visitors to Anfield were King George V and Queen Mary who attended the 1921 FA Cup semi-final between Wolves and Cardiff City. The reigning monarch Queen Elizabeth II has made a couple of visits to Anfield, her last being in 1993. The 1914 FA Cup final between Liverpool and Burnley was the first to be watched by a reigning monarch, King George V.

Other dignitaries include Neville Chamberlain, days after meeting Adolf Hitler in Munich during October

1937; Liverpool were beaten 2–1 on that day by Everton. Another prime minister to put in an appearance was Margaret Thatcher. Tony Blair visited the club while Labour leader, though not after his election to the top political office. Fellow party leaders Michael Foot and Neil Kinnock have paid visits on match day, as has one-time Tory leader Michael Howard in his capacity as a Liverpool fan. President Numery of Sudan, also a supporter, said his visit had great poignancy and shortly after, he paid for the club to visit his country and take on their top side, Al Nasr.

THIS IS ANFIELD

Those filing onto the pitch at Anfield must pass under a sign just above the tunnel's entrance. There is no precise information on when it was placed there, but there is sufficient evidence to narrow its introduction to some time during the 1960/61 season.

Shanks explained, 'It's there to remind our lads who they're playing for, and to remind the opposition who they're playing against.'

REALITY BITES

Former Liverpool players have been participants in a number of reality TV shows. A few years ago, Neil Ruddock entered the Australian jungle on *I'm A Celebrity Get Me Out Of Here*. Though an early favourite to win according to the bookies and a winner of ten stars in the first Bush Tucker Trial, he was the fourth evictee having lasted 11 days. He later managed a team of men with various problems as part of a series which aimed to turn lives around called *Saved by the Ball*, broadcast on Bravo. In a similar vein Glenn Hysen uses his experience as a coach on Sweden's *FCZ* show, which takes 15 non-footballers aged between 18 and 31, whom he then trains over the course of 16 weeks in order to get them into shape and play against a real side. 'FC Zulu' as the disparate band are known, play no less a club than 11 times national champions Djurgårdens IF – a side Hysen's son Tobias played for during the first two series.

John Barnes did better than his former colleague on lasting 8 weeks on the fifth series of *Strictly Come Dancing*. Performing with Nicole Cutler, he became the first ever male celebrity to score a perfect 10. Bruce Grobbelaar was expected to win *Hell's Kitchen* in 2009 but opted to leave 5 days from the end after deciding he wanted to be with his wife in South Africa rather than feeding dinner guests for chef Marco-Pierre White.

John Aldridge did a turn on the celebrity *X-Factor* type show entitled *You're A Star*. Aimed at raising funds for charity, it was broadcast on Irish television. Though far from the most gifted vocalist (he was actually rated the worst singer week in, week out), the decision was in the best traditions of reality TV based on public vote and those dialling in not only saved the striker each show, they selected him as their winner. Stan Collymore featured on Channel 5 show *The Farm* which saw well known names take on, well, farm tasks.

KOP IDOL

Not long before his sixteenth birthday, young Liverpool fan Thomas Tynan, a striker who had represented the city's schoolboys, entered a *Liverpool Echo*-backed competition to find a star footballer of tomorrow. He had only shown enough promise to make the county's junior grades and failed to be selected for the upper age ranges. He played for a modest local club, so was possibly not expecting much to come from the opportunity, but after collecting 20 tokens printed in the paper he got a trial – one of many held – and was quickly into the last 100 boys. When the number was pared down to a mere 20 he was in the final shake-up and invited to participate in some five-a-sides.

Two games were played and he grabbed five in each. Liverpool Football Club had dispatched their head of youth development, Tom Saunders, an acknowledged shrewd judge of talent, to the event. He didn't approach Tynan on the night but obtained the youngster's details and invited Tommy to train with the club. He jumped at the chance and was given terms after maintaining his impressive form and helping the club reach the 1972 FA Youth Cup final which the Reds lost 5–2 to Aston Villa. Within the year he had progressed even further and joined the reserves. However, that was as far as his career progressed and in 1976, without a first-team outing to his name, Tynan joined Sheffield Wednesday. It was with Newport County where he formed a partnership with fellow Scouser John Aldridge and Plymouth Argyle that he played most of his near 700 Football League appearances.

A SCORCHER FROM HOPKIN

Fred Hopkin, a recruit from Manchester United, could honestly say his first of a dozen goals for Liverpool set the stadium alight. Seconds after he netted the final goal in a 3–0 win over Bolton Wanderers in March 1923, the old Anfield Road Stand was ablaze. That capped his 78th appearance for the Reds. Smoke covered much of the field and threatened the game's completion with the second half no more than a few minutes old. Fortunately the fire brigade were able to deal with the problem and the patrons carried on watching in safety.

REDS ON THE SILVER SCREEN

There have been a number of references to the Reds on film. One of the most obscure was a deleted scene from *This Is Spinal Tap*. At a party held on the roof of a skyscraper to launch a tour, David St Hubbins is talking to Nigel Tufnel and offers this sage piece of philosophy:

''Cause it's like you're on the top of the world here, y'know, you really are. It's like the pinnacle. Y'know it's like when Dalglish is really on his game and he's away down the field and you know he's going to take them all away, 'cause he's on top of his game, y'know. That's how I feel.'

Tufnel suggests that Kenny is perhaps not the most fleet of foot and that Alan Hansen's wife is able to run faster. St Hubbins retorts, 'But Dalglish, y'know, he runs the first three yards in his head.'

The movie, as cut for cinemas, actually contains many footballing references, some extremely subtle, relating to Shrewsbury Town, Wolverhampton Wanderers and West Ham United.

SUPER REDS

In November 1977 Liverpool, as European Cup holders, took on Kevin Keegan's new side SV Hamburg – the European Cup Winners' Cup holders. A closely fought 1–1 draw in Germany was followed by a 6–0 hammering at Anfield as Liverpool cruised to a stylish 7–1 aggregate victory. Though Keegan spoke of finding a new challenge on the continent, he may have wondered how far his new team lagged behind his old one.

Just over a year later Anderlecht came up against the Reds for the right to call themselves Europe's super club. The Belgian side took the honours after a 3–1 home win and a 2–1 defeat at Anfield made it 4–3 in their favour over the two legs.

The trophy was decided by a single game in 1985. Juventus were hosts and made that home advantage pay with a comfortable 2–0 win.

As UEFA Cup holders, Liverpool challenged for the trophy with European Cup winners Bayern Munich a few weeks into the 2001/02 season. A 3–2 win allowed the Reds to claim a fifth piece of silverware in a little over six months. John Arne Riise, Michael Owen and Emile Heskey's goals were enough to ensure Liverpool won the game despite a spirited fight-back from the German outfit. CSKA Moscow were the first Russian side to participate in a Super Cup final, in 2005, but found European Champions Liverpool far too strong when the game went into extra time. Djibril Cisse grabbed an equaliser late on and, along with Luis Garcia, he also netted during the additional 30 minutes played.

HIGHER, FASTER, STRONGER

Liverpool-born Arthur Berry won two Olympic gold medals with the Great Britain football team. His first, while a student at Oxford University in 1908, was followed by another, four years later, when the title was successfully defended. He combined football with his legal studies and then practiced as a barrister. He was registered as an amateur Liverpool player for the first of those two Olympics but joined Everton during the 1912 games. Also in that squad was Ilford FC defender Joe Dines who made just one appearance for Liverpool soon after that triumph.

Great Britain have declined to field a team since 1964 in order not to come under political pressure from FIFA about the home nations each having an individual team, and a number of votes on key committees played its part in there being no further British Olympic football champions. The next serving Liverpool player to claim a medal of any hue was Javier Mascherano in 2008. The midfielder helped Argentina defend a crown he assisted them to win while at River Plate four years earlier. Emiliano Insua was named as a non-travelling reserve but wasn't needed. Lucas Leiva, who was selected to play for Brazil, won a bronze.

LONG AND DISTINGUISHED SERVICE

Players qualify for a testimonial after ten years' service with a club. Apart from Jamie Carragher and Steven Gerrard, who have already worn the red shirt in excess of a decade, there are few likely to do that and even the beating Scouse heart of the current Liverpool squad are long-shots to beat the mark set by Elisha Scott who enjoys an Anfield career lasting 21 years and 52 days, based on the time from first appearance to last. For the record those dates are 1 January 1913 and 21 February 1934. Carragher needs to play until at least the end of February 2020 – just beyond his 40th birthday – to reach that mark, and Gerrard should still be plying his trade at almost 42 years of age to rack up a stint of equal length.

JUST ONE BEFORE LEAVING ANFIELD ROAD

60 players have turned out for the club just once. Of that number Howard Kaye can consider himself particularly unlucky. He played over 150 times during the Second World War but as all these games were outside the Football League or FA structure he only ever made one official appearance – in a 3–2 home defeat to Blackpool in April 1947.

Joe Dines is another who only managed one game for the club despite playing in 27 amateur internationals. Keith Burkenshaw made his only Liverpool appearance towards the latter part of the 1954/55 campaign and was sold soon afterwards. However, that didn't stop him making a successful career at West Bromwich Albion and other clubs.

COME IN NUMBER 12, YOUR TIME IS UP

Some players didn't even get the chance of 90 minutes. Until recent times when various cup competitions have necessitated or at least lent themselves to the blooding of youngsters, only a few players had made just a substitute appearance but no more for the Reds. Kevin Kewley's only chance to grab the limelight came when he replaced Terry McDermott during a home League game with Middlesbrough in 1978. The Reds ran out 2–0 winners but Kewley never appeared on the team sheet again and had his contract cancelled soon after. UEFA's decision that anyone not qualified to play for the English national team was considered a foreigner in the early 1990s meant Graeme Souness had to dig deep inside the reserves to find Prescot-born centre half Barry Jones who got 68 minutes of a UEFA Cup tie with Finnish side Kuusysi Lahti. Brian

Mooney was given the last half an hour in the second leg of a League Cup tie with Fulham. Colin Russell made his only showing as a substitute for little more than 30 minutes in a disappointing 1–0 home defeat to Sunderland at the tail end of the 1980/81 campaign.

Those outings appear luxurious when compared to opportunities offered to others. But for extra time in a League Cup game, winger Mark Smyth would have had a career lasting just 21 minutes before joining Accrington Stanley. James Smith only has the final 16 minutes of a game in the same competition to look back on, while French goalkeeper Patrice Luzi has a few minutes less when replacing Jerzy Dudek in a 1–0 win over Chelsea early in 2004.

Antonio Barragan, who has a buy-back clause exercisable up to 2011, could still add to the 11 minutes he gained in a Champions League qualifier just 5 weeks after being signed from Sevilla in August 2005. However, that doesn't quite qualify to be the shortest career in Liverpool history. That dubious honour belongs to Miki Roque who was on the bench for the Reds' first return to Istanbul and the Ataturk Stadium just over a year and a half after the European Cup was lifted there. Galatasaray were the hosts and squeezed a win by the odd goal in five. Only 6 minutes remained on the clock when Roque replaced fellow countryman Xabi Alonso.

THEY SAID IT

'I don't like champagne, I don't smoke cigars, I haven't any real jewellery at all, apart from the 8 pieces of gold I picked up at Anfield; the most important relationship at a football club is not between the manager and the chairman, but the players and the fans.'

John Toshack

FRIEND OR FOE?

Many players have earned a reputation for putting in their best performances against Liverpool; something about the mere sight of a Liver bird can seem to inspire them to greater heights. However, the player to have scored most goals against the Reds is a familiar name on the Anfield team-sheet – Jamie Carragher with SEVEN own goals. Three have been to Tottenham's credit and one put West Ham United ahead in the 2006 FA Cup final. Ron Yeats, as big a figure at the back in the 1960s as Carragher is now, scored all four of the self-inflicted wounds Liverpool suffered between 1961 and 1967.

Putting through your own goal is an occupational hazard for any player. On one notorious occasion Avi Cohen wrote his name into Anfield folklore by jeopardising the certainty of the 1979/80 title. Needing a win to secure the crown, Liverpool were determined to claim the prize in the last home game of the season. A third-minute lead saw Liverpool take command until Cohen managed to push the ball past Ray Clemence just before the break. He looked distraught at the time, but only minutes after the interval he surged forward with an attack, finding himself in enough space unleash a low drive and restore a lead the Reds simply refused to let slip.

Thomas Cleghorn was the first Liverpool player to score an own goal on 27 December 1897 – something of a late Christmas present for the recipients Sunderland. A strange quirk of fate is that the Black Cats benefited from the initial five own goals conceded by Liverpool.

THEY SAID IT

'Talk to Carra, if you can understand him, you can understand anyone.'

Rafael Benitez to Fernando Morientes on his first day at Melwood

LONG-DISTANCE SHOOTING

Xabi Alonso became noted for his strikes from distance. The Spaniard scored against both Luton Town and Newcastle United when taking aim from inside his own half, and prompted by previous unsuccessful attempts, a Liverpool fan made a decent amount of money by placing a £200 bet on the possibility of a long-range effort prior to the 2005/06 season. With odds of 125-1 the lucky fan bagged winnings of £25,000. That said the midfielder isn't the most prolific marksman from distance . . . his fellow countryman Roger García notched three similar goals within 12 months playing for Espanyol. Garcia made all those efforts off his left foot, but Alonso was able to use both left and right.

A question often posed during the 1960s was this:

What's the longest distance a Liverpool goal has ever been scored from?

The answer is 8 miles. Sounds impossible? Yes, it is, but when Ian St John and Roger Hunt were in tandem and harassing defences, St John would often score from Hunt's cross. Hunts Cross, a district within the city of Liverpool, lies roughly 8 miles from Anfield. . .

who had come on as a substitute, edged Liverpool into the lead only for McCall to equalise once more. However, the club's best ever goalscorer had the last word with a deft header to make it 3–2.

Rush scored his fifth FA Cup final goal (a club and competition record) in 1992 to seal a 2–1 win over Second Division Sunderland. In a nervy, if often less than pulsating final, Liverpool faced Arsenal at the Millennium Stadium in 2001. After two defeats against the Gunners in finals, a balmy, sunny afternoon saw the Reds complete a cup double courtesy of late strikes from Michael Owen. The cup was won for a seventh time in 2006 when West Ham United were denied victory by an injury-time goal from Steven Gerrard. After extra time failed to produce a winner, penalties decided matters.

IT'S A NUMBERS GAME

Squad systems mean a player can literally wear any number, and ones which do not tie into their positions. For instance number one choice goalkeeper Pepe Reina turns out with 25 on his back. However, despite the somewhat strict enforcement of numbers relating to positions (number two is a right back, number three plays on the left-hand side of defence, etc.) the system was always voluntary.

Liverpool broke conventions many times. Tommy Smith, who after serving as a striker was pushed into a central defensive role, confused Anderlecht by wearing the number 10 shirt. The Belgians assumed he was an inside left – though possibly a deep-lying one and placed a man-marker on him. Half-backs normally wore the number 5 shirt throughout the 1970s and '80s, but it was another custom ignored. The central defensive pairing, as operated under the 4-4-2 system, wore 4 and 6, while midfielders, notably Ray Kennedy and Ronnie Whelan, wore 5.

The highest number held by a Reds player in the season squad numbers debuted (1993/94) was 25, worn by Neil Ruddock, which was appropriate to his then age, though Mark Gayle who was named as a substitute three times was handed the number 27 while on loan from Crewe Alexandra. Jack Robinson has the highest squad number ever recorded on a Liverpool shirt; he wore number 49 when introduced as a substitute late in the final game of the 2009/10 season.

The most worn numbers – each held by eight players since August 1993 – are 12, 18 and 22.

A HEAVY SHIRT TO WEAR

The shirt number which most Liverpool fans hold to be something approaching hallowed is 7. The man within it usually held the adulation of fans like no other, but again Liverpool broke the conventions. When shirts were first numbered it was customary for an outside right to don it. Ian Callaghan claimed the number on his debut and never really let go until Kevin Keegan arrived 11 years later. Though a midfielder when signed from Scunthorpe United, Keegan was asked to play in attack and the man who inherited the honour, not to mention his mantle in 1977, was Kenny Dalglish, who took the reputation of the number 7 to heights even his predecessor hadn't scaled.

As Dalglish eased himself upstairs and off the playing field, a few others tried the shirt on for size but the next custodian, Peter Beardsley, was one of the few who seemed anything like capable of carrying the torch he had been handed. Dean Saunders was next in line, then Nigel Clough who was the first player to hold the number under

AFTER HOURS

Everyone has to have a hobby which helps them to relax, including footballers. Golf would make for an easy list to compile and would include many names. There are very few trainspotters and stamp collectors among Liverpool's past and present ranks but there are still some interesting pastimes:

Kevin Keegan	bricklaying
Kevin MacDonald	gardening
Craig Johnston	photography and inventing, plus countless other activities
Mike Hooper	ornithology
David James	drawing
Frode Kippe	ski-jumping – he was a Norwegian champion as a youth
Javier Mascherano	pizza-making (at his brother's restaurant in Argentina)
Daniel Agger	tattoo artist

THE ONE AND ONLY

Many grounds have a stand known as the Kop, but only Liverpool FC and its fervent supporters are the club immediately identified with the word. And with some justification. Though the stand is now an all-seater grandstand catering for in excess of 12,000 spectators, it started life as a humble mound of cinders, earth and rubble in 1906. The board of directors decided those loyal fans that gathered in numbers up to 30,000 at the Walton Breck Road end of the ground who – even then – gave their all in support of the team, should be rewarded for their loyalty which had helped the club lift the First Division title for a second time. Though originally known as the Oakfield Road Embankment or Walton Breck Bank, local journalist Ernest Jones took one look at its imposing structure and christened it the Spion Kop. A huge hill of the same name had been a strategic post in the Boer War and was fitting in the respect that many local men had died attempting to defend it from the native South African forces. The site in Natal claimed a huge number of British casualties, though more than 300 were from Liverpool and surrounding areas.

Concrete was laid on top before a rebuild in 1928. The elements had poured down on fans for over two decades, but no more. Over 24,000 people squeezed beneath the new roof of a cantilevered stand which stood as the largest single-span spectator area in the English game measuring 425ft across, 131ft in depth and 80ft tall at its highest point. Fans gathered beneath to form a cathedral of worship for over six decades.

In 1989 it became an impromptu shrine over the hours, then weeks, after the Hillsborough Disaster. Many thousands of fans from clubs across the world paid their respects to those who died. The Taylor Report, which followed those sad scenes, recommended grounds in the top divisions be converted to all-seater stadia. The Kop had its last stand in May 1994 before making way for a new development.

THE OTHER LIVERPOOL

There is another club plying their trade under the name Liverpool: one from Montevideo, Uruguay, founded in 1915. Though their roots are very different from the one

of the Game, and in particular Law 10 dealing with The Method of Scoring, means such events would not lead to the registering of a goal. Additionally referees have powers to 'stop, suspend or abandon the match because of outside interference of any kind,' meaning the goal should have been ruled out and the match restarted with a drop-ball. They become outside agents and if the ball hits them or it is taken from a player, a drop-ball should ensue.

However, though these outside agents can be animate or inanimate, that didn't stop Liverpool conceding a goal against Sunderland to one of them in October 2009. Darren Bent's shot infamously struck a Liverpool-crested beach ball on its way past Pepe Reina, who would otherwise have made a simple save. Match referee Mike Jones, who seemed to have a clear enough view (so presumably saw the incident), didn't apply the law despite protests from Liverpool players. It was in truth a game the Reds didn't deserve to win based on performance, if not the circumstances.

AND THE REST IS HISTORY

Bristol-born Phil Taylor joined the Reds in 1936 and following the war was a member of the 1946/47 First Division championship-winning team. A centre forward who converted to a centre half, he also won England caps and played in the 1950 FA Cup final. After 345 appearances he hung up his boots and served as a coach, then replaced Don Welsh as manager in 1956. Taylor remains the only Anfield boss never to take charge of a top-flight game. He resigned in November 1959 having failed to lead the club back from the second tier.

A comment to the *Daily Post* proved telling. Taylor said, 'No matter how great has been the disappointment of the directors at our failure to win our way back to the first division, it has not been greater than mine. I made it my goal. I set my heart on it and strove for it with all the energy I could muster. Such striving has not been enough and now the time has come to hand over to someone else to see if they can do better.'

The man brought in to try to do just that was Bill Shankly.

LET THERE BE LIGHT

Liverpool installed floodlights on 30 October 1957 at a cost of £12,000. They were officially switched on for the first time by the then club Chairman Mr T.V. Williams. A specially arranged derby match was played to mark the occasion, which Liverpool won 3–2. Three weeks earlier the teams had met at Goodison Park to celebrate the installation of Everton's system. The initial pylon lights at Anfield were replaced by halogen bulbs attached to the stands in the 1970s.

SQUEEZING OUT OF THE GROUP

Liverpool share the record lowest points tally for qualification from a Champions League group with a paltry 7. Legia Warsaw were first to hit that mark and still progress in the 1995/96 season. The Reds were placed third in 2001/02, having not won a match in the second group phase until the tense last game meeting with Roma. At that point, a 2-goal win was needed after a defeat and 4 draws. Dinamo Kiev saw what a fickle finger of footballing fate can have in store when in 1999/2000 they made it out of the first group stage with 7 points but exited the next phase with a high-water mark of 10. Juventus and Lokomotiv Moscow, both

YOUNG STARS

Securing the vote as a League's best young player is an honour usually given to someone who has proved himself continuously over the course of a season against professionals with far more experience. Liverpool players have taken the award on 5 occasions. Three times it has been claimed by a striker with Ian Rush the first winner in 1983. Robbie Fowler was the next recipient 12 years later, and Michael Owen's goal-scoring feats in 1998 secured him the accolade in his first full season. One of the next young stars off the Liverpool production line, Steven Gerrard, enjoyed such a dominant season throughout 2000/01 that the then 20-year-old was touted as a possible candidate for the senior award. He gleefully accepted the PFA's Young Player of the Year award, though.

LIVERPOOL AGAINST THE WORLD

A club like Liverpool gets invited to take part in a number of high-profile friendlies and tours. Matches involving the club have taken part on every continent, but some of the more interesting games have involved non-club sides. The Irish Olympic XI used the Reds as a practice opponent on 19 August 1987 in Dublin. Liverpool were 5–0 winners. Other national teams Liverpool have played include Saudi Arabia in October 1978 when a 1–1 draw was fought out in Jeddah. South Africa, Great Britain, England and Ireland XIs have all provided competition at various stages. Israel have played the Reds twice in 1979 and 1983. With a win and a draw they remain unbeaten by Liverpool.

Thailand have played the Reds 3 times, the last being on a summer tour in 2009 when Singapore were also included in the itinerary. The Far East has long been a hotbed of support, but one only visited on a regular basis since the turn of the twenty-first century.

High-scoring friendly encounters include an 8–7 win over a Bury Select XI on 19 May 1982 and a 9–9 draw against a Bobby Charlton XI on 27 May 1977 in Tommy Smith's testimonial, held just 2 days after Liverpool won the European Cup for the first time. The Anfield Iron's service record will have attracted a large number wishing to pay their goodwill, but the presence of the trophy guaranteed a full house.

GET YOUR TRACKSUIT OFF, YOU'RE ON!

Before the advent of substitutes in 1965, a player being unable to continue meant those remaining would have to soldier on. Liverpool's first replacement from the bench was Geoff Strong, who came on for Chris Lawler in a home game with West Ham United on 15 September that year. He also became the first substitute to score when he squared the game at 1–1 half an hour after his introduction. In the modern game any 3 from 7 named players can be introduced. At that early stage just 1 could be called on and then only in the event of injury. The concept of tactical substitutions took some additional time to be accepted.

Steve Staunton is to date the only sub to score a hat-trick after coming on. He replaced Ian Rush at half time in a second leg League Cup tie with Wigan Athletic in October 1989. The Reds held a 5–2 lead from the opening game and though staged at Anfield, the game was officially an away tie; Springfield Park was deemed unfit to stage the match. Pressed into attack the Irishman, who was the night's only goalscorer, opened his account just before the hour and

marathon cup tie to yesteryear. Liverpool have had their fair share, including some of the most exciting on record, especially at the penultimate stage of the FA Cup. Amazingly the Reds have won none of them. In 1899 Sheffield United provided tough semi-final opposition. Liverpool held a slender 2–1 lead in the first game at Nottingham before succumbing to an equalising goal which set up a replay at Bolton's Burnden Park. It was a tense affair even if it ended in a sensational 4–4 draw. A second replay at Fallowfield failed to resolve matters when abandoned. It was poor luck as Liverpool led at the time. The Blades won the rescheduled match 1–0, denying Liverpool a first cup final appearance.

In 1962 Bill Shankly entertained his old side Preston North End in a fifth-round tie. The game finished goalless and the scoreline was repeated 72 hours later at Deepdale. Not even 30 minutes' extra time managed to separate the sides, so it was on to Old Trafford. The Lancashire club edged through and no doubt bruised Shanks' pride. Six years later and one round further on the road to Wembley, West Bromwich Albion were pitted against Liverpool. A 0–0 draw at The Hawthorns led to an Anfield return and a share in 2 goals. A 2–1 win in the second replay at Maine Road saw the Baggies through.

Though not a marathon tie, the 1979 semi-final with Manchester United was no less exhilarating and heralded the first of two titanic cup struggles in successive years. Maine Road was the neutral venue chosen, but a 2–2 draw necessitated a return at Goodison Park. The Reds couldn't find a way through after conceding an early goal.

Twelve months later Arsenal provided the opposition. Whichever team won through was a strong favourite to go all the way and lift the cup. Hillsborough saw them fight out a goalless draw, while 120 minutes of combat at Villa Park produced a 1–1 scoreline. Almost a fortnight later on the same ground, Liverpool left it very late when equalising with the last kick of the game. Hopes for a cup win were cruelly dashed in the fourth meeting at Highfield Road when the Londoners won 1–0.

League Cup marathons have been thinner on the ground. In 1984 Liverpool went on to claim the ultimate prize at Wembley but did so in a very laboured fashion. All but the second-round and semi-final ties, which were contested over 2 legs, needed replays to decide the outcome. Second Division Fulham put up strong resistance taking the League and soon to be European Champions to three games. Craven Cottage hosted the initial encounter which finished goalless. Fulham were pleased to have earned a money-spinning replay, but the prospect of dragging the Reds back to West London for another financially rewarding bite at the cherry after a 1–1 draw courtesy of a late penalty, raised hopes they could actually win through. The tie was finally decided by a strike close to the end of an additional 30 minutes in the third game.

In 1989 Liverpool and Arsenal were the country's top two teams. The early stages set up a mouth-watering clash with the potential to be equally as thrilling as the FA Cup semi-final encounter a decade earlier. Anfield hosted a tightly contested 1–1 draw. The Highbury replay was just as close and finished scoreless. A neutral venue was needed, and situated between the two cities, Villa Park seemed perfect. So was some of the football and at 1–1 with extra time or even another replay looming a winner was grabbed 3 minutes from the end.

GIANTS SLAIN

Perhaps the most humbling moment in Liverpool's FA Cup history came in 1959. Billy Liddell was dropped for the

THE ONE-UP CLUB

Despite hundreds, in some cases many hundreds, of appearances for the Reds, there are players who struggled to find the score sheet and have just one goal to show for their efforts in Liverpool's cause. Scoring isn't necessarily the best way to gauge a contribution, but a list still makes interesting reading.

Among the most notable members are Laurie Hughes, a veteran of 326 games who struck an 88th-minute equaliser against Preston North End and Gary Ablett, who notched in his second game for the club and his Anfield debut but failed to net in any of the remaining 145 games played before he joined Everton. Howard Gayle scored in a 1–1 draw with Spurs not long after a heroic display in the 1981 European Cup semi-final against Bayern Munich. As a result he found Liverpool's first goal in 270 minutes of League football.

Dick White spared blushes in the third round of the 1958 FA Cup encounter with lowly Southend United when he levelled the game and averted a very embarrassing exit from the competition. It set up a replay which the Reds won 3–2. Bobby Campbell was a loyal servant of 8 seasons, but he too just had a single goal to boast of when his Liverpool career ended.

A list of players to have made more than 50 appearances but have just one goal to their name is: Laurie Hughes (326), Dick White (217), Phil Babb (170), Archie Goldie (149), Gary Ablett (147), David Pratt (84), Nicky Tanner (59) and John McConnell (53).

TRADING IN

Not every player changes hands for huge or even modest amounts of money. Indeed, some can be transferred for a mixture of cash plus goods, or even just a pure trade of items – depending on the selling club's needs. There is often no definitive evidence of these alternative transactions, but Ronnie Whelan was rumoured to have fetched £35,000 plus a set of tracksuits for the squad when joining from Home Farm in 1979. Nicky Tanner was a player Liverpool invested £20,000 in when purchased from Bristol Rovers, but earlier in his career it is rumoured that when joining the Pirates from Mangotsfield United he was traded for a floodlight bulb.

KEEPERS OF THE FAITH

The list of great Liverpool goalkeepers reads like a Who's Who of the art. It is without doubt a highly specialised position and also one which enjoys a special place in the rich history of the club and usually in the hearts of fans. Many of the Reds' custodians, men such as Harry Storer, Ken Campbell, Elisha Scott, Arthur Riley and Cyril Sidlow, are just some of the names from the early part of the last century. These legends have been joined by Tommy Younger, Bert Slater, Tommy Lawrence, Ray Clemence, Bruce Grobbelaar, and Pepe Reina who have stood firm as the Reds' last line of defence.

Little wonder the club's telegraph address was GOALKEEPER.

THREE DECADES A LION

Emlyn Hughes is the only player to turn out for England in three separate decades. Gaining a debut in November 1969 against Holland, he played throughout the 1970s with his 62nd and final cap received in May 1980, a year after he had joined Wolves. A strange quirk is that despite an international career spanning almost a dozen years and three possible World Cup chances, Emlyn never made an appearance in the finals. He was in Alf Ramsey's 22-man squad in 1970 when England defended the trophy but failed to play and his country did not make it out of the qualifiers in 1974 and 1978. Ray Clemence, with 61 caps, also failed to feature in a World Cup finals game as he played second fiddle to Peter Shilton throughout the Spain 1982 tournament.

There is one player with an Anfield connection who can beat Hughes' feat. Jari Litmanen made his debut for Finland against Trinidad and Tobago during the latter months of 1989. When he took to the field in January 2010 against South Korea – the same nation his 100th cap was earned against – he had played international football in four separate decades. Though a Champions League winner, he too has never played in a tournament finals as the Huuhkajat have yet to reach these stages of any major competition.

WILDERNESS YEARS

Though he gained a cap during the group stages of the 1966 World Cup and only spent the final looking after Nobby Stiles' teeth, Ian Callaghan has the medal FIFA belatedly decided to honour those who didn't manage to get a game with. Cally also has the longest intervening period between caps at 11 years and 49 days. A second was won when Alf Ramsey selected him for duty against France on 20 July 1966. A third cap came against Switzerland on 7 September 1977 under Ron Greenwood. A fourth and final England outing was earned almost five weeks later against Luxembourg in October.

Liverpool players often made up the backbone of England squads. Greenwood selected 6 for his first match in charge – that game against Switzerland. It may be a reason why Cally got the call up. The 5 who joined the then 35-year-old were Ray Clemence, Phil Neal, Terry McDermott, Emlyn Hughes and Ray Kennedy. Kevin Keegan may be considered a selection which extended an Anfield nucleus, as he had only moved from Liverpool to SV Hamburg during the preceding summer.

DRAFT-DODGING

If Mohamed Sissoko were to be believed he would have one more Mali cap than the record books show. Following a World Cup qualifier against Senegal in September 2005, the then Valencia midfielder stated there was still a friendly to play with Kenya. On being asked about the game when returning to Spain, Sissoko said he had played 48 minutes of a 1–0 win and felt fine. It later transpired he had been visiting his ill father in a Paris hospital. Manager Claudio Ranieri excused the subterfuge when the truth came out, telling Sissoko he could have had the time off. Whether such deceit would have got past Rafael Benitez either at the Mastalla or Anfield is unlikely. If the game was on, Benitez would have known and made time to sit in front of it with a note pad.

DODGY KEEPER?

Stephane Henchoz has never played as a goalkeeper but cynics suggest the Swiss international may have excelled at the role and that he would not even have needed gloves. He made apparent saves, and potentially match-winning ones, against Arsenal and Manchester United at the Millennium Stadium in the 2001 FA Cup final and Community Shield respectively. On each occasion the officials decided any handball wasn't intentional or simply missed them, but TV replays forced even the most ardent Reds to accept there may have been a bit of arm or hand in there.

A LOAD OF OLD TOSH

Autobiographies fill the sporting sections of bookshops and though there are a few instances of players writing fiction – often related to the game – only one has been in print as a poet. John Toshack had a volume of rhymes and odes entitled *Gosh It's Tosh* published in 1976 by Gerald Duckworth & Co. Ltd.

Said to have been inspired by Muhammad Ali and with Kevin Keegan providing an on-field muse, there is a sporting if not literary pedigree to the tome which can fetch high prices on the second-hand book market. There are references to not just the game but Liverpool Football Club as well as the beauty of his own country – Wales. Over three decades later a second volume has yet to be penned. Toshack qualifies his work by stating his prose are 'in the main, meant to be light-hearted.'

TRANSFERS

Liverpool's transfer kitty has rarely stretched enough to land players for a domestic record fee. Only the capture of Stan Collymore from Nottingham Forest in the summer of 1995 has ever made the Reds the country's biggest spenders. Kevin Keegan and Ian Rush attracted record fees when they joined SV Hamburg and Juventus respectively.

Almost a decade after a player first changed hands for £1 million, the Reds broke that ceiling when landing Peter Beardsley. That set a record mark between British football clubs – though fees from continental clubs were always far higher. Dean Saunders joining in 1991 increased the mark between English clubs, though at a time when the record reached £30 million Emile Heskey was Liverpool's first ever eight-figure sum player and his £11 million fee remains comfortably within the ten highest-priced purchases.

The top five transfers are listed below, though are notional as in some cases deals are undisclosed and have involved the writing-down of fees owed for players previously sold to a vending club. Liverpool sold Robbie Keane back to Tottenham for £16 million.

1	Fernando Torres	£20.2m
2	Robbie Keane	£19.0m
3	Javier Mascherano	£18.6m
4	Glen Johnson	£17.5m
5	Alberto Aquilani	£17.1m

TEENAGE KICKS

At 17 years and 129 days Max Thompson had been the youngest player to turn out for Liverpool, making his debut soon after the Reds won the FA Cup in May 1974. Though a central defender he was a replacement for striker John Toshack who was injured at Wembley. His giant 6ft 4in frame may explain the reason he came in. The match with Spurs at White Hart Lane ended 1–1 and completed the League programme. As it turned out, Thompson became one of Bill Shankly's last selections. Bob Paisley kept an eye on Thompson who was a regular for the reserves but gave him just one outing as a substitute in the UEFA Cup against Real Sociedad before sanctioning a switch to Blackpool in December 1977.

Jack Robinson played out the closing moments of Liverpool's 2009/10 season replacing Ryan Babel at Hull City's KC Stadium. It was a bright spot in a relatively dull 0–0 draw. Just 16 years and 250 days old, he only had academy experience and bypassed the reserves. Indeed, he had only trained at Melwood once, before being drafted in due to a chronic list of injuries across the back line.

Michael Owen, who made his debut in May 1997, missed Thompson's mark by a mere 15 days when gaining his debut as a substitute against Wimbledon, but became the club's youngest scorer when netting late in a 2–1 defeat. The striker was an unused substitute against Sunderland in a tense win at Roker Park three weeks earlier. If deployed by Roy Evans he would have claimed the then record.

Phil Charnock became the youngest Liverpool player to take part in a European game when he replaced Steve Harkness in a European Cup Winners' Cup tie with Apollon Limassol on 16 September 1992. He was 17 years and 7 months old at the time. Six days later he started a

League Cup match with Chesterfield. The tenderest player to sign for Liverpool or any other Football League club is Ray Lambert who joined the Reds as an amateur in January 1936, a mere 189 days past his thirteenth birthday. He signed professional terms just before the outbreak of war a little over three years later and may well have exceeded the records subsequently set had he not had to wait a full 7 years to make an official appearance for the first team.

COMING THROUGH THE PACK

It is often said that being top at or around Christmas is the key to a successful title bid. There have certainly been very few examples of successful charges from a club too far off the pace during the festive season. However, as the last of the turkey was being placed in sandwiches during 1981, Liverpool lay in 12th position and some points off the pace but, partly due to having a couple of games in hand, surged through the campaign's final months to take the crown with some comfort – 4 points ahead of Ipswich Town.

SUCCESS IN OTHER FIELDS

A number of well-known people and household names hoped to make the grade as professional footballers only to follow another path when it became clear they would not be good enough. Liverpool's list of nearly men include comic Stan Boardman who played a few youth games but ultimately rose to nothing more than celebrity XI status. Another one was Derek Acorah, who now professes to see dead as well as red people in his role as a psychic medium; he was an apprentice during Bill Shankly's reign under his given name of Derek Johnson. With that moniker he served Wrexham, Glentoran, Stockport County and Australian outfit USC Lion as a professional. A knee injury forced his retirement. Perhaps he should have foreseen that, too?

X-FILES

Although there are few reports of ghoulish behaviour at Anfield, if an interesting tale is to be believed Liverpool were certainties to lift the Worthington Cup in March 2001 once Birmingham City got through to the final. It was allegedly all thanks to powers beyond this realm. The story goes that when Birmingham obtained the land St Andrews was built on in 1906, aggrieved Romany people who had used it until that time placed a curse on the club. The hex stated that the Blues would never achieve success. Attempts to lift the curse have been made which include ex-manager Barry Fry urinating in each corner of the pitch. 95 years on and despite a strong effort, the Midlanders remained without a trophy to their name after losing the penalty shoot-out.

It may also be that fate was always going to smile on the Reds given that Liverpool are one of the few clubs to have a Romany on their books. Rab Howell played for the club between 1897 and 1901 making 68 appearances.

STILL STANDING

Though the old Kop terrace was demolished and sold off in chunks to raise money for charity, an item remains from the developments in 1928. That is the wooden topmast of the *Great Eastern* ship – one of the first vessels made of iron anywhere in the world. When the blueprints were on Isambard Kingdom Brunel's drawing board, it was the largest ship ever scheduled to be built. Salvaged from a breakers' yard it was floated across the Mersey via Rock Ferry. Once the mast reached its destination, four horses carried the huge pole up the Everton Valley and to Anfield where it was erected at the corner of the Kop and Kemlyn Road stands. This place has been known as Flagpole Corner virtually ever since.

It had first set sail in 1858 taking passengers and cargo across the Atlantic, including trips from Liverpool. Later she laid communications cables across the same stretch of water, then saw out her days as a showboat offering pleasure cruises of the Mersey and acting as a floating advertising hoarding for John Lewis's department store in the city. Before finally being sold for scrap in about 1890, much of the iron had been used in the building of a funfair at Liverpool's Royal Jubilee Exhibition three years earlier. It had been left to rot for over two decades when the mast was purchased.

A BLESSED TRAINING GROUND

The open spaces of West Derby made it a prime area for the construction of a training ground in the 1950s. Liverpool chose a piece of land situated on Melwood Drive. The area was previously owned by St Francis Xavier's School and had been used as a playing field. Though other sports were practised there it was somewhat appropriately best known as a football venue and derives its name from a tribute to each of the priests who spent many hours overseeing sessions there – Father Melling and Father Woodlock.

TREBLE CHANCES

But for a freak goal which cannoned off Jimmy Greenhoff's chest during the 1977 FA Cup final, Liverpool may have celebrated a treble of the game's three ultimate prizes. The League Championship was secured before Wembley and the European Cup 4 days after that disappointment. It took the Reds a further 7 years to secure three trophies from a single season for a first time when the League title, European Cup and Milk Cup were claimed in Joe Fagan's first season as manager. Gerard Houllier had been employed a little longer when Liverpool became the first English side to win three knockout cups in the same campaign. Without a trophy in 6 years, the Reds treated themselves to both domestic prizes on offer, plus the UEFA Cup. All were won in thrilling circumstances. A penalty shoot-out in the Worthington Cup came before a couple of late goals, after the Reds trailed Arsenal, secured the FA Cup and a sudden death own-goal during extra time against CD Alaves brought a first European trophy in 17 years.

WHOSE SIDE ARE YOU ON?

Injury is something of an occupational hazard for a footballer, but usually fitness will be jeopardised by an opponent rather than a team-mate. There are, of course, exceptions. Just five days before the 1988 FA Cup final Nigel Spackman and Gary Gillespie went up to deal with a high ball forward against Luton Town. A clash of heads ensued. Fortunately both made the Wembley showpiece courtesy of stitches and rather fetching matching protective headbands.

Fixtures and fittings have troubled players more rarely but perhaps the most notable was the time Phil Babb tried to stop Pierluigi Casiraghi slotting into an unguarded net when Chelsea came to Anfield in October 1998. The Republic of Ireland international attempted to slide in and divert the ball behind, but on a slightly greasy surface couldn't control his movement and, legs akimbo, collided with a goalpost. He was substituted soon after and didn't return to the match squad for over a month. Ouch.

A HEAVYWEIGHT RECRUIT

Legendary World Heavyweight Champion Joe Louis, who ruled the division for a dozen years until retiring in 1949, would probably have made a more fearsome defender than Neil Ruddock or Tommy Smith and proved far more rugged a midfield hardman than Graeme Souness, Paul Ince and Steve McMahon put together. Despite 'signing' for Liverpool during a tour to entertain British troops in 1944 'the Brown Bomber', or Private Joe Louis as he was known during the war, did not pull on the famous red shirt and test any of the above claims due to his recruitment being nothing more than a publicity stunt for both club and 'player'.

CODED MESSAGES

The signing of Terry McDermott just after his Newcastle side lost in the FA Cup final to Liverpool owed much to some veiled hints and a not-so-subtle code between two lads from Kirkby. Phil Thompson was injured in September 1974, and while in hospital recuperating from an operation he was contacted by Bob Paisley who asked what he knew about the midfielder. Thompson had to admit very little other than they hailed from the same part of Merseyside and had swapped shirts at Wembley.

Paisley confessed he would like to bring him to Anfield. With only modest telephone communication available at the time, Thompson wrote a letter talking about the manager's comments while attempting not to make it look like an approach was being made on the club's behalf. The return post was less restrained. McDermott confessed a move to Liverpool would be 'his dream'.

The Liverpool manager asked that a message be relayed to his target pleading that he sit tight and not do anything 'daft', though after a few weeks McDermott wrote back to Thompson keen to learn of any developments. It was soon after that his name became linked with his boyhood team. A few more missives changed hands before a £175,000 deal was agreed between the clubs. Thompson and McDermott became friends and roomed with each other for many years after.

SCORING FEATS

Although Cyril Done scored 7 against Chester during 1943, and both Bill Shepherd then Don Welsh hit 6 in convincing victories over Wrexham and Southport respectively, these feats were achieved in wartime games. On two separate occasions in a little over 3 months during the First World War, Thomas Bennett scored 5 goals. However, as far as the record books are concerned none of these efforts officially count, which leaves the highest number of goals scored by a Liverpool player in a single game at 5.

William Miller   v Fleetwood Rangers (7–0) Lancashire League
3 December 1892

Andy McGuigan	v Stoke City (7–0)	Division One
		4 January 1902
John Evans	v Bristol Rovers (5–3)	Division Two
		15 September 1954
Ian Rush	v Luton Town (6–0)	Division One
		29 October 1983
Robbie Fowler	v Fulham (5–0)	Coca-Cola Cup
		5 October 1993

Roger Hunt scored 100 goals in the fastest time, taking a mere 144 matches. Fernando Torres brought up his half-century in 72 games when scoring against Aston Villa in December 2009. In doing that, he beat Albert Stubbins and Sam Raybould to the mark by 8 matches, and should he maintain the ratio, would reach Hunt's tally in the same number of games.

Hunt holds the record for most League goals in a season with 41 during the 1961/62 season. Ian Rush could not beat that number in his Division One outings, but did claim 49 from all competitions in 1983/84. The striker claims it should be 50 as he scored in the penalty shoot-out with Roma which won the European Cup final.

I RUN THE LINE

Jimmy Hill saved a Liverpool game at Highbury from being abandoned in September 1972 by swapping his commentator's microphone for a flag and replacing an injured linesman. Dennis Drewitt was forced to withdraw and without a reserve official, the only hope was to find a qualified referee somewhere in the ground. The call was answered by the former professional. The game finished goalless with no complaints about Hill's decision making.

KING KENNY COULD HAVE BEEN CROWNED EARLIER

On 20 August 1966 Kenny Dalglish turned out for Liverpool's 'B' side in a game with Southport which completed a one-week trial. A 1–0 win was registered and Dalglish, who wore the number 8 shirt, returned home. There had been positive feedback but the interest wasn't followed up. West Ham United were also content to send him back to Scotland with nothing more than their best wishes and a brand new pair of boots once the chance to extend his stay with the Hammers was rejected. During the week Kenny was at Upton Park he was invited to watch the home game which coincided with his trial – a home clash with Liverpool.

APPEARING ON THE SCORESHEET

When Liverpool beat Crystal Palace 9–0 in September 1989 a record 8 different players managed to get on the scoresheet. This is the first and only time so many players have netted in the same top-flight game. Steve Nicol got the opener after just 7 minutes and scored the last during the closing seconds. Between those two strikes Steve McMahon, Ian Rush, Gary Gillespie, Peter Beardsley, John Aldridge, John Barnes and Glenn Hysen beat the seemingly hapless Eagles' stopper Perry Suckling.

Aldridge, who hurriedly took his training gear off when the referee awarded the penalty, scored with his first touch after replacing Beardsley. The striker was joining Real Sociedad the next day and this 23-minute cameo was to be his farewell. To this day no other player has ever been introduced in order to take a spot-kick. Geoff Thomas missed a penalty for the visitors. Just to show how a season can have as many swings as roundabouts, Palace knocked Liverpool out of the FA Cup at the semi-final stage.

Bruce Grobbelaar may have fancied taking a spot-kick in that 9–0 mauling. The Zimbabwean had done so for Crewe shortly before arriving at Anfield, but he along with David Burrows and Alan Hansen, were the only men not to beat Suckling. In September 1974 no fewer than 9 different scorers were on the mark when Liverpool beat Norwegian outfit Strømsgodset at Anfield in a Cup Winners' Cup tie. Ray Clemence had little to do on the evening with Brian Hall the only outfield player not to find the net.

REDS RUNNING RAMPANT

Liverpool's record wins in each competition are:

League	10–1	v Rotherham Town	Division Two 18 February 1896
FA Cup	8–0	v Swansea City	second-round replay 9 January 1990
League Cup	10–0	v Fulham	second round, first leg 23 September 1986
European Cup	10–1	v Oulu Palloseura	first round, second leg 1 October 1980
Fairs/UEFA Cup	10–0	v Dundalk	first round, first leg 16 September 1969
ECWC	11–0	v Strømsgodset Drammen	first round, first leg 17 September 1974

SAME GOING BACKWARDS

A member of Liverpool's youth team from the early part of the 2000s is the only professional player to have a palindromic name – Leon Noel reads the same backwards as forwards. A bustling striker with pace, Noel was tipped to do well and could play on the wing if required. However, he failed to make the professional game and played at amateur standard with Warrington Town and Crossfield-Rylands FC.

THEY SAID IT

'At a football club, there's a holy trinity – the players, the manager and the supporters. Directors don't come into it. They are only there to sign the cheques.'

Bill Shankly

'If you're in the penalty area and don't know what to do with the ball, put it in the net and we'll discuss the options later.'

Bob Paisley

'If Shankly was the Anfield foreman, Paisley was the brickie, ready to build an empire with his own hands.'

Tommy Smith on the Bootroom dynasty

'Sometimes I feel I'm hardly wanted in this Liverpool team. If I get two or three saves to make I've had a busy day.'

Ray Clemence on the art of an Anfield goalkeeper

THREE LIONS – THREE RED CAPTAINS

Michael Owen was named England's vice-captain by Sven-Göran Eriksson and, with David Beckham absent, he led his country out for a friendly with Serbia and Montenegro in June 2003. As was customary with the then national manager, a host of substitutions were made before the game ended. Owen was one of those withdrawn and had three successors to the armband. As the game was at Leicester City's Walkers Stadium, former Foxes player Emile Heskey took over. He was followed by Jamie Carragher, meaning a trio of serving Liverpool players had led England in the same match. Before the end Phil Neville also took over. It was the first time four players had captained England in a single game.

THE SEASON'S BEST SIDE – ON PAPER

When Liverpool won the 1963/64 League title they were not allowed to parade the silverware. Even though it sat just under half a mile away in Everton's trophy room, the 'Old Lady' as it was known due to the design, could not be couriered across Stanley Park. The Blues did offer, but only when the result was known as both they and Manchester United still had an outside chance of pipping the Reds before the victory over Arsenal put everything beyond mathematical doubt. If Everton could hang on to the prize there was no prospect of it being taken away from Goodison.

There were also protocols in place, namely that the Football League had to retake guardianship and then officially present the silverware. If it was not to be after the title-clinching game or another match that season, it had to take place behind the scenes. Therefore, the

League rather than Everton, would not yield and as the only games which remained were on the road, the Anfield board were reluctant to be presented with the trophy at the midweek game with Birmingham City. Consequently a papier mâché alternative – though far from an exact replica in red and white – featured in pictures of the title winning team.

A CHAMPION AND RELEGATED IN THE SAME SEASON

Mark Lawrenson set a record in 1988 which has yet to be equalled. The Irish international was forced to retire by a persistent Achilles problem and took over as manager of First Division strugglers Oxford United in late March. His fourteenth and last appearance of the season for Liverpool in January had been enough to qualify him for a championship medal. Oxford were relegated after gathering just 31 points – 59 fewer than Liverpool – and finishing rock bottom. Lawrenson, who failed to win a single League game after taking the reins at the Manor Ground, became the subject of many pub quiz questions as the man who won a title and got relegated in the same season.

SHOULD HAVE WON ON POINTS

Liverpool have contested a world title three times. Though endorsed by the respective governing bodies, an unofficial version known as the Intercontinental Cup pitted the Champions of Europe against their South American counterparts – the Copa Libertadores holders. The Reds lost heavily to Brazilian outfit Flamengo in 1981 but were narrowly beaten 1–0 by Argentine club Independiente 3 years later. Though able to pit their wits against South America's finest on another two occasions, Liverpool opted not to take part in 1977 and 1978 due to a heavy domestic schedule. Boca Juniors would have been the opponents both times.

FIFA officially sanctioned a tournament from 2000 and organised a structure with representatives from all the respective confederations. São Paulo beat Liverpool in the 2005 final but the result could and should have been very different. The Reds had 3 goals disallowed: Luis Garcia and Florent Sinama-Pongolle for debatable offsides. Sami Hyypia converted from a corner which the linesman ruled had gone out of play before reaching the giant Finn. Overall Liverpool had 21 shots and 17 corners. The woodwork was also struck twice and Harry Kewell was virtually wrestled to the ground in the area – yet no penalty was given.

A LEAGUE OF NATIONS

When Liverpool started the Premier League era, Ronnie Rosenthal was the only Anfield employee from outside the British Isles to feature in the opening game, and that was as a substitute. Across the Premiership just 10 players from outside the home nations and Ireland started games at the beginning of that term. Before the Reds ended that season the Israeli international was joined by two Danes, a Norwegian, a Hungarian and a Zimbabwean. Over the seasons to have elapsed since, that list has grown exponentially. All continents of the globe have since made their mark – with varying degrees of success – on the squad. No fewer than 30 separate nations have had players turn out for Liverpool in the League since August 1992. 11 Spaniards are within the total number, but that is overshadowed by the number of French players, which totals 15, including French-born Nabil El Zhar and Mohamed Sissoko who play for Morocco and Mali respectively.

The four international federations of the United Kingdom have been able to select from a rich pool of talent at the club. Harry Bradshaw was the first man from Anfield to turn out for England when Ireland visited Nottingham on 20 February 1897, an easy 6–0 win for the hosts. George Allan was the first Red to don the dark blue of his homeland when Scotland took on their oldest foes, England, at Crystal Palace on 3 April 1897. George went back to Anfield a happy man following a 2–1 win for his side. Maurice Parry had to settle for a 1–1 draw when Scotland visited Wrexham on 2 March 1901 becoming the Reds' first Welsh international when the country of his birth awarded him a cap.

Before Northern Ireland and the Republic went their separate ways in 1924, players would turn out for Ireland. The first man to do so was Bill Lacey on 18 January 1913 when Belfast hosted a 1–0 win for Wales. The first man to play for the newly formed Northern Ireland was Elisha Scott. Wales were the opposition once more and Elisha kept a clean sheet.

ON FOREIGN FIELDS

Liverpool have played official games in 33 countries and many more when friendlies are included. Matches within England and Wales have come as part of the domestic programme. The Reds have also played in these nations:

Germany	17	Japan	4
France	15	Switzerland	4
Spain	14	Austria	3
Italy	11	Poland	3
Belgium	8	Denmark	2
Portugal	8	Norway	2
Wales	8	Republic of Ireland	2
The Netherlands	7	Czech Republic	1
Scotland	7	Iceland	1
Finland	6	Lithuania	1
Greece	6	Luxembourg	1
Romania	6	Northern Ireland	1
Russia	6	Slovakia	1
Hungary	5	Slovenia	1
Turkey	5	Sweden	1
Bulgaria	4	Yugoslavia	1

WARTIME INTERNATIONALS

During the war, Victory and Wartime Internationals took place. Jack Balmer and Ephraim Longworth turned out for England while Scotland called upon the services of Matt Busby, Willie Fagan, Jim Harley and Billy Liddell. Ray Lambert and Robert Matthews were selected by Wales.

HOW DID I DO?

The princely sum of £500 exchanged hands between Liverpool and Chesterfield for Sam Hardy, a keeper who a few months earlier had visited Anfield for the first time and conceded 6 goals. His performances for Liverpool suggested that game was either a temporary blip or simply down to the team he was facing. Hardy certainly proved himself worthy of the huge fee invested in him for the times, spending half a dozen happy seasons on Merseyside and claiming a championship winners' medal in his debut campaign after ousting Ted Doig from the keeper's jersey.

Doig had endured a torrid run of form and results which threatened to jeopardise the team's challenge. A storming end to the previous term when Liverpool claimed the Second Division title by some distance had many tipping Liverpool to follow it up with the English title, but five defeats within the opening eight games left that bold prediction floundering. As can happen, Doig lost confidence, allowing his understudy a crack at the first team. It was a chance he refused to pass up easily, and with Hardy in goal Liverpool finally began to string some results together, starting with a 4–1 win against Nottingham Forest on 21 October 1905. The title was claimed by 4 points.

SCORELESS

In 243 games Rob Jones failed to find the net for Liverpool, despite being a rampaging full-back for much of his Anfield career. He did everything but score though; missing by inches, striking the woodwork several times and seeing efforts spectacularly saved by goalkeepers. Jones was on the mark twice with his previous club Crewe Alexandra, but excluding goalkeepers, is the Liverpool player with the most appearances never to find the net. Stephane Henchoz, a rare visitor to opposition penalty areas, is the next in line with 205 barren outings.

INTERNATIONAL BOSSES

Matt Busby, Kevin Keegan and John Toshack are former Liverpool players to have managed home international sides. Busby, who also took charge of the 1948 Great Britain Olympic squad, spent 3 months at the helm with Scotland a decade later. Keegan managed England for a brief spell, and Toshack, who was in charge of Wales for just 41 days during 1994, ended up taking on the same job almost half a dozen years later. Peter Cormack had a stint as Botswana's national coach. Steve Staunton, the holder of 102 Republic of Ireland caps, had 17 games in charge of the team soon after retiring.

WORLD CUP REDS

Laurie Hughes was the first player to take the field in a World Cup while on Liverpool's books. He made 3 appearances for England during the 1950 tournament, including a shock defeat by the United States of America. Anfield has had at least one representative at all but one World Cup finals since, although until South Africa 2010 only Roger Hunt had been a winning finalist.

Ian Callaghan and Gerry Byrne were members of the victorious England squad in 1966 but did not play against West Germany, while Dietmar Hamann was a runner-up with Germany in 2002.

There were Liverpool players on both sides of the 2010 final when Spain played Holland. Dirk Kuyt started the game with Ryan Babel an unused substitute. Both had to be content with runners-up medals as Spain pulled off a tight win. It took extra time to separate the sides. Liverpool's Fernando Torres came on at the break in that additional period, playing a part in Andres Iniesta's winner, while Reds keeper Pepe Reina kept a watching brief from the bench. Former Reds Xabi Alonso and Álvaro Arbeloa were also in the Spanish squad.

LEAGUE LEADERS

Liverpool's Football League record is predictably impressive. Up until the Premiership's formation, the Reds had won more games than any other club. From the 3,524 matches played, victory had been tasted 1,650 times with 851 draws and 1,023 defeats. 6,071 goals had been scored in the process with 4,527 conceded. The largest points haul from a single season in any campaign is 90, achieved at the close of the sensational 1987/88 term. This equalled the then overall record which Everton had set. When wins only earned 2 points, the Reds collected 68 from a possible 84 in 1978/79.

CHIPS OFF THE OLD BLOCK

It may sound incredulous but Emlyn Hughes named his two children – a girl and a boy – Emma Lynn and Emlyn.

MODELS OF CONSISTENCY

21 players have played more than a century of games without interruption. Phil Neal, who missed just a handful of matches he was available for throughout a 12-year stay, did so twice. Emlyn Hughes and Bruce Grobbelaar also notched up a run of more than 100 games twice. Neal's record would have been bettered but for an injury against

Manchester United in September 1983 which led to him missing the next game. Within his tally are 366 League games and without that enforced break the record Tranmere Rovers' Harold Bell set of 401 games in the competition would have been broken.

Phil Neal	417	David James	213
Ray Clemence	336	Alan Kennedy	205
Bruce Grobbelaar	317	Ian Callaghan	185
Chris Lawler	316	Kenny Dalglish	180
Emlyn Hughes	177	Roger Hunt	120
Peter Thompson	153	Emlyn Hughes	108
Tommy Smith	152	Dick Forshaw	106
Elisha Scott	132	Bruce Grobbelaar	106
Robbie Fowler	129	Steve McManaman	106
William Goldie	129	Jimmy Melia	105
Phil Neal	127	Ron Yeats	102
Gerry Byrne	120	Tommy Robertson	100

OLDEST RED

Ted Doig enjoys an unusual place in the record books. He is the oldest player to turn out for the Reds at 41 years and 165 days on 11 April 1908. He is also the oldest Reds debutant making his bow just under three and a half years prior to that 53rd and final game for the club. He had previously spent 14 seasons with Sunderland.

Billy Liddell is the club's oldest goalscorer. He earned that accolade when netting the third goal in an easy 5–1 win over Stoke City at the grand old age of 38 years and 55 days.

Until Doncaster Rovers chairman John Ryan made a contrived appearance for his side in the last minute of their final Conference game in 2003, aged 52 years and

11 months, one-time Liverpool man Neil McBain was the oldest man to have turned out in a competitive game. When he was manager of New Brighton, the then 52 years and 4 months-old McBain, a former half-back, fielded himself as an emergency keeper in a Division Three North game against Hartlepool United in 1947.

THE KIDS ARE ALRIGHT

Many of the club's great players have come from within the ranks, having graduated through the youth system. A purpose-built academy was opened in Kirkby to nurture junior talent in 1998. Over 56 acres of land, it boasts a dozen floodlit pitches, including 4 which are full-size, as well as indoor facilities and state-of-the-art equipment. Liverpool have managed to claim the junior grade's premier knockout competition, the FA Youth Cup, on 3 occasions. All these wins have taken place within the past 2 decades with the last couple being successive triumphs from 2006 to 2007. The first triumph took place in 1996. The Reds were defeated finalists in 1963, 1972 and 2009.

ALMOST A RED

A host of players have at one time or another been courted by Liverpool managers only to see a deal fail to materialise. Perhaps the most intriguing tale is that of Frank Worthington. The then Huddersfield Town forward was a hugely talented player but also a notorious womaniser. Bill Shankly was an admirer of his on-field activities and wanting to complete a team he knew would challenge for the title, made his move. A fee and personal terms were agreed but a medical scuppered the signing. Frank's blood pressure was too high. Worthington blamed it on his test being carried out by an attractive nurse. Shanks reasoned that a relaxing break may be what was needed and told him to come back after a holiday when the procedures could be repeated. That was a fine theory for a rested body and mind but Frank went to Majorca – a renowned Mecca for thrill-seekers and night-clubbers – maintaining his regime of booze and late nights with a Belgian woman he met over there. A second medical was failed. He joined Leicester City – one of 24 League and non-league clubs he served.

A PROGRAMME OF SHARING

For over 50 years Liverpool and Everton shared their match day programmes. Until 1904 this took the form of a simple card listing the expected line-ups and rest of the season's fixtures. The team not playing at home would chart the progress of their reserves on the flip side. A programme similar in nature to modern-day editions was published after this date. Usually consisting of 24 pages it also detailed the day's teams and League fixtures as well as general items such as theatre reviews and adverts. The front cover had a football with Everton written across it. The other edge also had a football on it, but this time bearing the name of Liverpool. In 1905/06 when the Reds won the League and Blues the FA Cup, the cover featured a player from both camps shaking hands. Each was holding their respective piece of silverware.

The First World War saw the programme reduced to a single folded piece of paper. It returned to a booklet-style effort following the Allied victory, even if a little lighter in page numbers. When the clubs decided to print their own programmes in 1934, it created more room for in-depth features on players and games. At this time Liverpool started to put photographs on the front cover. The programme has kept pace with the rapidly increasing upturn in affluence and the quality of technology available.

THE LONG . . .

Though a number of towering players have turned out in a red shirt, Peter Crouch, who had lived in Macclesfield, London and Singapore by his fifth birthday, is by far the tallest at 6ft 7in. The forward needs his jerseys and shorts to be specially extended. He is also the loftiest man to ever represent England.

. . . AND THE SHORT OF IT

The most diminutive player to play for Liverpool is Sammy Lee who at 5ft 2in is 17 inches shorter than Crouch. In 1975 the boyhood Reds fan achieved a long-held dream after signing apprenticeship forms at 16. He made his first-team debut in April 1978 after a number of impressive displays in the youth and reserve teams earned him the chance. A player bursting with energy and passion, he was always a crowd favourite and remained so even after leaving the club due to a lack of first-team opportunity in 1986. He has served in coaching capacities at Anfield under the last four Liverpool managers and took charge of the side in December 2008 when Rafael Benitez was recovering from treatment to remove kidney stones.

Emiliano Insua is the shortest man currently plying his trade at Anfield and the joint smallest in the Premier League, with Aaron Lennon, at 5ft 5in.

WHAT YOU TALKING ABOUT, AVI?

Avi Cohen became a notorious figure and a firm piece of Anfield folklore. On his first day of training he used a peg in the dressing room next to that of Kenny Dalglish. Avi was, as far as many were concerned, the only non-English speaker. Cohen himself didn't really seem to have accepted that, and over and over again he would tell Dalglish, 'Me, you, same.'

The Scottish forward merely nodded politely at first, but after further repeats, finally asked his new colleague what he meant. 'Kenny, you, me, same,' Avi said. 'Both learn English.'

MILESTONE GOALS

Liverpool have scored a total of 7,210 League goals. The milestone strikes are as follows:

1	Malcolm McVean	v Middlesbrough Ironopolis	2 September 1893
100	Tom Bradshaw	v Sheffield United	8 December 1894
500	Andy McGuigan	v Wolverhampton Wanderers	9 November 1901
1,000	Jack Parkinson	v Sunderland	12 April 1909
2,000	Gordon Hodgson	v Bury	29 December 1928
3,000	Kevin Baron	v Everton	24 December 1949
4,000	Roger Hunt	v Sheffield Wednesday	8 December 1962
5,000	Kenny Dalglish	v Wolverhampton Wanderers	25 March 1978
6,000	Jan Molby	v Derby County	23 March 1991
7,000	Mohamed Sissoko	v Sunderland	25 August 2007

HEADS ... YOU WIN

In September 1946, Liverpool were looking to sign Tommy Lawton but in the hours following a 5–0 defeat to Manchester United, they were rebuffed by Chelsea, despite the prospect having seemed open when talks had begun with Stamford Bridge officials a few weeks earlier. The process of luring Newcastle's Albert Stubbins began quickly. So acute was the need for a centre-forward, that immediately on arriving back in Liverpool from Maine Road – Old Trafford was bomb damaged – the club chairman and manager George Kay drove straight to the north-east. Everton, who were also interested in the player, got wind of this and followed their counterparts up the A1. Stubbins had taken his wife to the cinema that evening but having received word that Newcastle wanted to contact him, made his way out of the picture house early. On reporting to St James' Park, he met officials of Liverpool and Everton but decided he would not push the nose of either suitor out of joint, tossing a coin to decide who he talked to first.

If he liked what he heard there would be no need to speak to the rival. Liverpool were lucky enough to get the first opportunity, and with the personal terms to his liking, Stubbins shook hands on a deal. It was also felt that a club tour to America, where Stubbins had spent some years as a youth, was a huge piece of bait. So, too, a column with the *Football Echo* arranged by the club. Goodison officials went home once it was announced an agreement had been reached.

TAILS . . . YOU LOSE

On the theme of tossing coins . . . Liverpool's first European campaign included a draw against Cologne of West Germany who played out a couple of scoreless games which necessitated a replay at a neutral venue. Rotterdam hosted that meeting – a 2–2 draw. No further replay was scheduled and penalties were not used to decide matches at the time. Progress would be decided by nothing short of luck. A disc, one side white, the other red, would be tossed. The captains picked colours meaning should it land with the appropriate red sector facing up, Liverpool would progress to the semi-finals. Ron Yeats always savoured a 50/50, but was nervous about this one as players and officials stood in the centre circle to watch the referee throw the disc high into the air. However, there was no reaction from anyone when the disc landed as it had managed to stick in mud on its side! Deciding the toss to be inconclusive, another was made. This time there was a definite result and a Liverpool win declared.

Unfortunately, Yeats was not so lucky three years on when Athletic Bilbao tied with Liverpool in a European Fairs Cup meeting. Both legs ended 2–1 to the home sides, though Liverpool's goals in the second game at Anfield came late. It may have been hoped that their luck would be in after such an ending. Yeats, who this time was asked to call a real coin while it was in mid-air, shouted tails. On exiting the pitch he was immediately met by his manager who asked him what had happened. Ron told him, only to have the manager bark back, 'Christ, you should have said heads! I don't know why you picked that!'

INSULT TO INJURY?

Tommy Smith had a deserved reputation as a hard man, though was only booked once in his career. That yellow card came during a Cup Winners' Cup second-round tie against Ferencvaros. Liverpool played the opening leg at Anfield and had a slim lead until Máté Fenyvesi found an equaliser in the last minute. Out in Hungary, Liverpool just couldn't manage to find a goal and late in the game Smith was accused of feigning injury and pretending to have been hit by a missile. The referee brandished a caution.

TWO TROPHIES ON THE SAME DAY

Liverpool's 1946/47 title was secured without kicking a ball when Sheffield United beat Stoke City a fortnight after the Reds concluded their programme. The season had been delayed by extremely bad winter weather with the Blades more acutely hit than most. Liverpool were due to play Wolves in April but that game was postponed due to the Reds' FA Cup involvement, so became last match of their season. A win at Molineux put Liverpool top while Stoke trailed by a point before kicking-off their final game. The Potters were the only team potentially able catch the Reds. Not much may have been expected as Sheffield United were just seeing out their season and had no need for the points, but the Blades didn't let anyone down and secured a 2–1 home victory. On the same night Liverpool were playing Everton in the Senior Cup final which kicked off 15 minutes later than originally scheduled to allow the players to get news from Bramall Lane prior to the final whistle in their own game. When affairs in Yorkshire ended, the referee stopped the game at Anfield and allowed the players to receive the news. On confirmation of the top spot being retained, all Liverpool's players were congratulated by the Everton men. The game restarted after the plaudits had concluded and the men in red had congratulated each other and saluted the 40,000 fans present who also celebrated a Liverpool win on the night.

Two trophies were physically placed into Liverpool's hands when the Reds successfully defended the League Cup in 1982, 1983 and 1984. The Milk Cup, as the trophy had become known, had a piece of silverware minted but the old three-handled trophy on offer since the competition's inauguration was also passed to the club. Captain on that day, Graeme Souness also lifted two trophies when Liverpool won the Football League in 1983 as inaugural sponsors Cannon commissioned a golden trophy to be handed out alongside the traditional accolade which Liverpool retained in 1984 then regained in 1986.

FOOD FOR THOUGHT

Sports scientists and nutritionalists who ensure players have all the fuel and assistance needed to produce their very best are commonplace in the modern game. But it wasn't always so, and certainly not at Liverpool Football Club. It only changed when Graeme Souness, who had played in Italy and saw the benefits of a good diet, took charge at Anfield. Foods such as fish, pasta, chicken and rice were the type of foreign cuisine men like Bill Shankly eyed with suspicion. So too Ian Rush, despite a season with Juventus. When asked why 'delicacies' like cheese toasties and beans (among other things) had been stopped, Souness suggested it was to ensure the side would play better. To which Rush is rumoured to have retorted, 'But boss, we won the double on egg and chips.'

BILL OF FAYRE

Bill Shankly was a popular man both on and off the pitch. Soon after he retired, the players organised and paid for a dinner in his honour. The menu was specially constructed to represent the man and his passion for the club he had served over a decade and a half. A picture of Shankly sat on a menu which listed starters, main course and a dessert. The meal began with clear Mersey soup then moved on to cured Kop cod.

A LONG WAIT FOR A BIG MAN

Of the list of strikers to have played for Liverpool since the Second World War, Peter Crouch has waited the longest to notch his debut goal. It came in his 18th game, against Wigan Athletic, and 1,229 minutes into his Anfield career. For the club alone that represented almost 21 hours of football but when a few goal-free England outings were factored in, the wait for a goal had lasted more than 24 hours. That mark passed 11 minutes in to the Wigan game. The wait could well have been 13 minutes longer – or maybe some point beyond that as the goal seemed to settle a very visible anxiety Crouch was toiling under. However, a shot which looped in off Leighton Baines and was palmed in rather than over by keeper Mike Pollitt, proved to be a huge monkey off his back. Though initially designated as an own goal it was credited back to the forward on appeal.

Crouch may be the only player whose wait has reached four figures, but some came perilously close to the same landmark, including the club's most prolific marksman Ian Rush who waited 813 minutes to find the net. Michael Robinson had much expected of him though didn't enjoy a level of success comparable to the Welshman – except in the regard that he required 29 minutes fewer to grab his first goal. Jack Balmer, a fine servant and a man who indulged himself in the goals, took 531 minutes.

THEY SAID IT

'Who's bigger than Liverpool?'
Jamie Carragher when asked if he ever thought of moving to a bigger club

QUICK OFF THE MARK

By complete contrast to that list are those who have scored on debut. To the close of the 2009/10 season 86 players have completed that feat. Of course that includes the 5 men on target when Liverpool made their bow in the Lancashire League. Throughout the early part of the twentieth century, goal times were not recorded accurately enough to be sure who took the fewest minutes to hit the net. However, Billy Millar, who scored with just a touch more than a minute on the clock against Bury in August 1928, is probably the quickest. That goal came in the first game played before the newly roofed Kop. Michael Owen, who beat Neil Sullivan within 16 minutes of being introduced as a substitute at Selhurst Park against Wimbledon in May 1997, holds the record for those emerging from the bench on debut.

ON THE SPOT

Liverpool players have successfully converted 456 penalties, excluding shoot-outs. Over the years there have been many great penalty-takers able to keep their cool and grasp the advantage a spot-kick brings. Few were more fearsome to the facing goalkeeper than Jan Molby, who leads the way with 42. A laid-back style of play possibly made him a natural choice. The Danish international, who missed just 3 penalties, is one of a dozen players to reach double figures and the only player to net a hat-trick only from spot-kicks, in a League Cup tie with Coventry City in November 1986.

Phil Neal, who is second on the list, would have topped his former team-mate had he converted just a fraction of the 13 chances he managed to spurn. Michael Owen and Tommy Smith are the only other players to reach double figures for misses.

Jan Molby	42
Phil Neal	38
Billy Liddell	34
Tommy Smith	22
Steven Gerrard	21
Robbie Fowler	20
John Aldridge	17
Terry McDermott	16
Gordon Hodgson	15
Michael Owen	13
Kevin Keegan	11
John Barnes	10

PAYING THE PENALTY

A missed penalty against Cardiff City in April 1954 effectively consigned the Reds to relegation. The Bluebirds had earlier needed to replace regular keeper Ron Howells, victim of a broken thumb, tasking Alf Sherwood – a man Stanley Matthews declared to be his hardest opponent – to take a turn between the sticks. The defender, who was a stand-in at both club and international level, faced the fearsome Billy Liddell, who at that stage had been unsuccessful with just 3 of his spot-kick attempts, but Sherwood managed to save not only the kick, but a follow-up too. Cardiff won 1–0. Just 2 games remained and the failure to grab at least a point – another may have followed if the game had been levelled – sealed the club's first term outside the top flight in 50 years.

THE SHOOTISTS

Until the 2009/10 season closed, Liverpool have been involved in 11 penalty shoot-outs, losing only once. That misfortune came in a League Cup tie with Wimbledon on 14 December 1993. Five trophies have been won via this method of deciding a contest.

A list of shoot-out wins is as follows:

10 August 1974	Leeds United	Charity Shield won 6–5
30 May 1984	AS Roma	European Cup final won 4–2
13 April 1992	Portsmouth	FA Cup semi-final won 3–1

18 January 1995	Birmingham City	FA Cup third round won 2–0
25 February 2001	Birmingham City	League Cup final won 5–4
4 December 2002	Ipswich Town	League Cup fourth round won 5–4
1 December 2004	Tottenham Hotspur	League Cup fifth round won 4–3
25 May 2005	AC Milan	Champions League final won 3–2
13 May 2006	West Ham United	FA Cup final won 3–1
1 May 2007	Chelsea	Champions League semi-final won 4–1

A FACE IN THE CROWD

Albert Stubbins, who represented Liverpool for a number
of seasons after the Second World War, is the only
footballer among the cultural icons featured on the cover of
The Beatles' 1967 album *Sergeant Pepper's Lonely Hearts
Club Band*. Situated towards the middle on the third row,
the striker stands between George Bernard Shaw and Sri
Lahiri Mahasaya. George Harrison is close to hand on his
right. Hunter Davies, author of *The Glory Game*, has been
a ghost writer for a host of sports memoirs and was acting
as the band's official biographer when he suggested that
a footballer should be included somewhere in the cut out
figures ordered and designed by artist Peter Blake. Though
he retired in the 1950s and died aged 82 in 2002, Stubbins
has a well-subscribed Liverpool FC fan club named in his
honour and was used as a character for Stephen Baxter's
novel *The Time Ships*.

DID THEY HIDE THEIR FOOTBALLING LOVES AWAY?

On the question of The Beatles' footballing allegiance, author of the book *This Is Anfield*, Andy Thompson, asked Ringo Starr and surprisingly found he was an Arsenal fan due to his London-born stepfather taking him to the homes of both Reds and Blues when the Gunners were in town. However, the drummer's two sons are rumoured to own Anfield season tickets. Paul McCartney's dad was an Everton fan and Paul, who was pictured outside Wembley before the 1968 FA Cup final sporting a blue rosette, certainly followed that tradition. Later in the year on a photo shoot for The Beatles' *Mad Day Out,* he wore a Liverpool rosette. He now claims to indulge in that unholiest of activities – supporting both sides – claiming his affections come mostly through personal friendships with Anfield players during the 1970s. Paul's brother Mike is a Red.

George Harrison and John Lennon were not huge fans of the beautiful game, though George's son Dhani shouts for Liverpool. When asked by journalists, Harrison, who was rumoured to have attended the 1957 FA Cup final between Aston Villa and Manchester United, seemingly preferred to tantalise with his answer, 'There are three teams in Liverpool you know, and I prefer the other one.' As AFC Liverpool didn't exist at the time, it is likely he was dismissing his inquisitors out of hand, or suggesting he was a regular at Holly Park the Garston home of South Liverpool FC. John is said to have attended the 1950 FA Cup final. Although there is little substantive proof, we can work it out – if anything his leanings were Red.

1966 AND ALL THAT

Statistically the first goal in a cup final is crucial. More often than not teams who grab a first goal hold their advantage. Few teams manage to come from more than a goal down. When Liverpool achieved the feat in the 2006 FA Cup final, coming through despite trailing 3–1, they were the first team to do so since Everton beat Sheffield Wednesday after trailing 2–0, 40 years earlier. The Reds were facing that level of arrears from the 28th minute.

RHYTHMIC REDS

Various events in Liverpool's history, plus players, have provided inspiration for band names. The 25 of May celebrate Liverpool's historic first European Cup win over Borussia Mönchengladbach on that day in 1977 – though the Reds of course also won the trophy on the same date in 2005. Croydon-based St Etienne took their name from the club Liverpool famously beat in the 1977 European Cup quarter-final – though not due to the tie. Ian Rush, a Welsh band, took their eponymous name from the principality's legendary striker. Though unsigned to a record label they have a decent internet fanbase.

DUAL NATIONALITY

FIFA outlawed the practice of 'changing allegiances' in 1960. Even though it wasn't an easy thing to do in the governing bodies' eyes, far too many professionals were adopting new countries to win caps. It is now only allowed in certain circumstances, and of course in the event of a once-established nation splitting into two or more parts – as has happened throughout Europe since the early 1990s. Irish players were legitimately allowed to switch between Northern Ireland and the Republic before 1950. Bill Lacey represented Northern Ireland between 1909 and 1924 then Ireland from 1927 to 1930, adding three caps to the 23 initially earned. Gordon Hodgson turned out once for his native South Africa against the Netherlands in Amsterdam in 1924. Although recognised as a national appearance, South Africa's Football Associations were fractured along racial lines and with the country a dominion of the United Kingdom, the Springbok team were essentially touring amateurs. It was in this capacity that Hodgson came to the attention of Anfield scouts. Just under half a dozen years later he was making his debut for his adoptive nation – England.

Tommy Smith didn't actually add to his sole England cap against Wales in 1971, though he did represent Team America as a midfielder for the USA Bicentennial Cup Tournament in matches against Brazil and England. The peculiar-sounding XI cobbled themselves together from North American Soccer League players at a time when Smith played for Tampa Bay Rowdies.

BALL-BURSTING BILLY'S LIDDELL PIECE OF HISTORY

Shots on goal are often said to burst nets if only in a metaphorical sense, but Billy Liddell's second in a 3–2 win over Tottenham Hotspur literally appeared to have done just that. However, on inspection it was discovered that the effort had only disconnected the netting from the hooks attaching it to the goal's frame. Just under 3 years on, the winger popped a ball – but not with his feet. Against Fulham, a blistering header flew at the Cottagers' keeper like a bullet, but cleared the crossbar by just a few inches. Fans returning the ball into play suggested the referee take a look, indicating it had burst. The official agreed. It wasn't unusual for Liddell to split a ball open, such was the might of his shooting, but many suspected that a header doing similar damage as one of Billy's boots was a first for the Anfield legend. Even towards the end of his career those ferocious powers hadn't waned. In his seventh to last of the 534 matches he played for the club, he hit a shot with so much venom that the ball burst with a bang so audible that it would not have seemed out of place on bonfire night.

THEY SAID IT

'My secretary, Sheila, was right in line with the shot and she says it was a goal. That's good enough for me.'
Rafael Benitez speaking after the goal against Chelsea in the 2005 Champions League semi-final

'This is Anfield, they say you'll never walk alone . . . it's true!'
Rafael Benitez

STRIKING IT RICH

Ever wondered who sat on the Pools Panel? And, in the case of postponed games, who could net punters a multi-million-pound jackpot? The first panel was formed in 1963 primarily due to an Arctic winter causing the postponement of matches for a number of months. In order that the pools industry didn't fall – three successive coupons had already been wiped out – a commission of experts was formed. Some of the game's great players; Tom Finney, George Young, Tommy Lawton and Ted Drake, sat on 26 January that year. Since the mid-1970s ex-Reds striker Roger Hunt has been a panel member sitting in Liverpool along with Tony Green and another World Cup-winner, Gordon Banks.

Spot the Ball was a game used by newspapers where participants would place crosses on a picture hoping to identify exactly where the centre of the ball was in still images taken from a game. That would be decided by an expert panel on which Ian Callaghan has sat for many years. His hero Billy Liddell was also one of those who offered an opinion. He retired when Alzheimer's Disease started to affect his judgment. It was unusual for participants to be 100 per cent accurate, so the top prize would rely on closeness. If there were a number of successful entrants a machine which magnified the area would determine which cross was placed nearest.

TRIBUTE TO A LEGEND

Just under a year after Bill Shankly's passing, the Shankly Gates were unveiled on 26 August 1982. They were a simple tribute to a man who took a club from Second Division mediocrity to the heights of the European game, and, even if he couldn't personally win the Champions Cup – Kings of Europe. Shanks' widow, Nessie, formally unlocked the gates before a small crowd of invited guests and a ceremony attended by club chairman John W. Smith, captain Graeme Souness and Bill's successor, Bob Paisley. The words 'You'll Never Walk Alone' are across the top of the wrought iron structure. Situated at the junction of the Anfield Road End and the Main Stand, they are filed under by millions of fans every season.

LIVER BIRD

This mythical creature has been the central part of Liverpool Football Club's badge for over 100 years. The suggestion is it made a first appearance on a Liverpool shirt in 1901, though it has been an official symbol of the City of Liverpool since 1797. Visitors make a point of viewing the two huge statues designed by German wood carver Carl Bernard Bartels above the Royal Liver Building on the Pier Head. It's a sight which for some defines the city's skyline. At the time of Liverpool FC's formation, clubs had a habit of borrowing the emblem of their town or city for a crest. As the team bore the same name as the city, adopting the Liver Bird must have seemed a natural choice. The winged creature which looked rather similar, once inhabited the Mersey Basin area.

However, as far as experts are concerned there is absolutely no evidence that the Liver Bird ever existed. Theories as to its origins include that it may be the eagle adopted by King John of England, as he chose the once small fishing village of Lerpoole as the base for his campaigns in Ireland during the early part of the thirteenth century. It is also believed that it could be a cormorant. When Liverpool was officially created as a borough, the coat of arms included a bird very similar to the cormorant, and they are known to have nested around the port area. In its beak was a piece of seaweed. Laver, being an old English word for seaweed, could conceivably have derived the word liver.

American writer Herman Melville, author of *Moby Dick*, made mention of the Liver Bird in his novel *Redburn*. He had been influenced by a guidebook he read on a visit to Liverpool in 1839.

PAISLEY GATEWAY

In order to pay tribute to the most successful club manager in the history of the domestic game, Bob Paisley, Liverpool Football Club commissioned the production of a pair of wrought iron gates at the Kop end of the ground. They were opened on Thursday 8 April 1999 by Bob's widow, Jessie, just over three years after his sad death. Other family members present were Bob and Jessie's sons Robert and Graham, plus daughter Christine. Bob's brother Hughie and his wife Mary travelled from the north-east.

Mrs Paisley had taken quite an influential role in the design of the tribute, along with architects Atherden Fuller Leng, to ensure the gates were as representative of Bob not only as a manager but as a person, and received a ceremonial key. The entire process took over 18 months to complete. Standing 4.5m high and weighing over 2 tonnes, they are quite a work of art and feature three European Cups in the archway to signify the triumphs Bob guided the club to in 1977, 1978 and 1981. The crest of his birthplace, Hetton-le-Hole, is prominent on the left-hand side gate (as someone approaching the ground from Walton Breck Road would see it), and features a steam engine to acknowledge its role in the early development of the railway industry and mining. A Liver Bird plaque is on the right. Four footballs surround both crests. On either side of the gates two brick pillars bear bronze reliefs created and designed by artist Jim Cooper. They depict an image of Bob and the honours he won during nine seasons. The foundations at the point they were erected had to be specially reinforced.

MASTERS OF THE GAME

Supported by the Professional Footballers' Association, Sky TV and a host of companies, retired players and one or two veterans still plying their trade at various levels of the game can partake in a Masters tournament. The competition has been arranged every year since 2000. Played during the summer there are regional competitions, then a national final. Those participating – usually on an annual basis – read like a who's who of the club. Liverpool are the most successful side in the tournament with 6 regional championships and 2 national final wins in 2001 and 2002. Though times have been a little lean recently, the grand final evening is usually reached and in 2006 the Reds won a prestigious tournament against teams such as Manchester United and Chelsea in Dubai.

ON SECOND THOUGHTS

It's often argued that as a referee never changes his mind, there is no point arguing with him. On one occasion, though, it didn't take outraged Liverpool players crowding Spanish referee José-María Garcia-Aranda to alter a decision to give Roma a penalty when Markus Babbel clearly handled 10 minutes from time in a UEFA Cup tie. Liverpool held a 2–0 advantage from the opening leg in Italy, but with Michael Owen having already missed a penalty they were hanging on to the aggregate lead. Just 10 minutes remained and extra time would have promised more of the same had the visitors not actually gone on to grab a third. It was at the Kop end and whether that affected the official who was suddenly signalling a corner is unknown. Señor Garcia-Aranda later said he had never given a penalty.

DUSTING OFF HIS BOOTS

Graeme Souness took pride in his fitness. Good conditioning allowed the Scot to play until 37. He had officially hung up his boots before becoming the Reds' manager but caused speculation about a return by turning out in a reserve match against Aston Villa in October 1991.

BRIEF ENCOUNTERS

It isn't only those with just one appearance who can play a minimal amount of time. Jean-Michel Ferri gained 47 minutes over the course of the two substitute outings he made. German international Sean Dundee spent a season at Anfield. At a £2 million cost – mitigated by half the sum being recouped when he left – the forward contributed 44 minutes after three introductions from the bench.

SHOULDERING THE BURDEN

Former Liverpool reserve Michael Stensgaard was forced to retire after dislocating a shoulder when putting up his ironing board which fired up an old injury. The then 21-year-old Danish keeper hadn't got further than the Anfield subs' bench but was able to make a return after medical treatment and help from canoeist Arne Nielsson – an Olympic silver medallist. He went on to play in his home nation's top flight as well as spending a season at Southampton.

THE GREATEST GOAL NEVER SEEN

In a Liverpool shirt Jan Molby scored three goals against Manchester United. Though they were far from his favourite team in terms of hitting the target, the Dane reserved one of his best ever efforts for the Old Trafford outfit. It came in a Milk Cup game at Anfield during late November 1985 and was the first in a brace which turned the game around after Paul McGrath provided the visitors with a lead. The build-up began with a midfield tussle. Molby made a stiff challenge on Norman Whiteside just before the hour. Rather than look for the pass he just kept running. Three defenders were brushed off as 'Big Jan' raced in to the danger zone and unleashed a shot from 20 yards. The ball flew in like a bullet and despite having a clear sight United keeper Gary Bailey didn't have time to react. Virtually motionless, he could do no more than watch it cannon into the roof of his net.

However, due to a strike by TV workers only the 41,291 present plus officials and players saw it. That was until late in 2009 when a tape surfaced. It was broadcast by the club's in-house channel in a show featuring interesting relics from the club's past. For almost a quarter of a century between, Molby had stated he held a cassette in his loft but had simply not dug it out. Legend is that police cameras were responsible for capturing the image, but Old Trafford manager Ron Atkinson is actually the man to thank. He hired someone to record the game from the Main Stand gantry to analyse later. His side hoped to be vying for the title. The footage has allowed a few holes to be picked in a tale which has seen the number of players beaten and range of the shot increase.

NAME GAMES

Some of Liverpool's past and present players have some
very unusual and often distinct middle names. Six of the
most curious are:

Peter BARR Cormack
Emile William IVANHOE Heskey
Paul EMERSON CARLYLE Ince
Glen MCLEOD COOPER Johnson
Larry VALENTINE Lloyd
Mark EVERTON Walters

MAKING A SPECTACLE

Long before they could opt for contact lenses as a method
or gaining full vision, players would have to struggle or
wear their spectacles. Centre-half Alex Raisbeck is believed
to have been the first to don glasses on a regular basis.

HOUSE WARMING RUINED

Liverpool were the very first visitors to Old Trafford on 19
February 1910 and came from 3–1 down to earn a win by
the odd goal in seven.

GOOD OMENS

Ahead of the 2005 Champions League final some interesting
coincidences between that year and others Liverpool had
claimed the European Cup were found. The most intriguing

link was for 1981 when the Reds beat Real Madrid in Paris. Also Prince Charles got married. So did Ken and Deirdre in Coronation Street. Liverpool finished fifth in the League and a new Dr Who arrived on the screens. All those things came to pass before Liverpool edged AC Milan on penalties. Manchester United fan Christopher Eccleston must have been proud of the part he played by agreeing to play the Gallifreyan Time Lord in its small-screen comeback.

THE BIGGEST JOB IN CLUB FOOTBALL

It's fair to say Roy Hodgson split opinion when appointed as Rafael Benitez's successor in July 2010. The Reds had spent almost a month without a manager, although the man who led Fulham to a Europa League final was always a favourite in the boardroom. Like all Anfield managers he will receive the unqualified backing of the fans who he probably won over with his opening comments at the press conference to announce the news.

'This is the biggest job in club football and I'm honoured to be taking on Britain's most successful football club,' the 62-year-old said.

THE LAST WORD

'A lot of football success is in the mind. You must believe that you are the best and then make sure that you are. In my time at Liverpool we always said we had the best two teams in Merseyside, Liverpool and Liverpool reserves.'

Bill Shankly